Klara

Claire Arndt

Copyright © 2017 by Ingrid Boozer
All rights reserved.
ISBN: 1545180210
ISBN-13: 978-1545180211

CONTENTS

	Acknowledgements	i
Chapter One:	Flight Out of the East	1
Chapter Two:	Youth in the Reich	21
Chapter Three:	Blossoms of Spring	39
Chapter Four:	The War Begins	59
Chapter Five:	Bielany	73
Chapter Six:	A Tearing of the Heart	97
Chapter Seven:	Collapse and Flight	115
Chapter Eight:	Ashes Across the Sky	125
Chapter Nine:	Strange Events and Last Days	143
Chapter Ten:	Homecoming	155

ILLUSTRATIONS

Klara Schulrabe	Front cover
Sisters Klara, Aline and Hilda	41
Klara as queen of the ball, 1938	56
Melsungen Heilstatte Stadtwald	58
Klara, Hilda, Aline 1939	62
Kassel after October 1943 RAF raid	71
Warsaw streetcar 17 to Bielany	86
Aline Maria Otto Klara Hilda 1945	129
Dresden after Feb. 1945 firebombing	141
Schulrabe family in Melsungen	166
Postcard of Melsungen Sanatorium	Back Cover

ACKNOWLEDGMENTS

I would like to thank all those who listened and helped to write down these memories, particularly Woody Carlson, my granddaughter Ingrid and my daughter Ruth who saw this project through to completion. Some details of conversations have been improvised to bring my early years to life, and some names of people have been changed for their privacy, but the events and relationships described in these pages do reflect my true experiences during the first quarter-century of my life.

Klara

Chapter One
FLIGHT OUT OF THE EAST

Our train was a tiny speck, lost in the vast flat prairie of the Ukraine. I looked out through the window of our coach. Fields rushing past beyond the rail embankment proved we were moving, though I no longer noticed our coach swaying or the pounding iron wheels beneath us. When I lifted my eyes to the horizon the sense of motion almost vanished. It looked exactly the same as it had for hours.

My family sat in silence all around me. Little Aline slept beside me, her pale hair cascading over my shoulder. She felt warm against me in the drafty coach. Looking down at her brought me echoes of her crying from hunger in the winter. In our long, empty brick farmhouse we had huddled together through the endless short days and long nights of the Russian winter, alone and tiny in the vast snowy landscape. Now that world receded behind us forever with every clack and rumble of the moving cars.

"What do you see out there, Klara?" asked Otto. I looked around to meet my brother's eyes. My thoughts wouldn't form at once into words so I only shrugged my shoulders. Beside him my other sister Hilda daydreamed in her own private silence. I tried to choose the most important of the thoughts straying across my mind. They all harked back to the winter.

"I was thinking about the day we walked from the farm into Starie Karan, to see Papa in that place," I told him at last. That was one of the thoughts circling each other in my head as I sat staring from the train. How could I forget such a day? The prison buildings seemed ugly and frightening to me from the first moment I saw them. We sat on the snowy ground outside while Mama went in. Russian soldiers stood all around. We were so hungry! That I remembered particularly.

Papa frowned. What had he been thinking about? Was it my remark to Otto? His eyebrows knitted together the way they did when something disturbed him. Mama looked out the train window as if to spy a remedy for our unpleasant memories in the bleak expanse of fields and prairie. For a moment an impression of loneliness overwhelmed me. Despite our nearness in the compartment I suddenly felt alone. Each of us seemed cut off from the others, lost in private thoughts about some unknown future, blank and confusing.

The moment passed. Our train rattled on, carrying us farther and farther north, away from the only home I had ever known. For thirteen years I had lived in that long red brick house, secure in the cycle of the seasons and my family.

No, not for all thirteen years. Actually the troubles had gathered like storm clouds for three years, starting in 1930. Have you ever seen a thunderstorm build up on the prairie? At first only a long grey line of clouds rises on the horizon—a hint of trouble. But with astonishing swiftness the leading clouds come rushing across the sky. Thunderheads tower up higher and higher, smother the sunlight, fill the air with oppressive stillness.

Working far out in the fields, there is no time to find shelter. Suddenly thunder crashes. The sunshine gives way to shadow. Great dirty raindrops come pelting down. Lightening leaps from heaven to earth, testing and probing. The storm roars down as you run away from the wagons and throw yourself down in the warm black soil. The horses rear and snort, crazed with fear. They break the traces and run wildly away.

More than once, caught in such a storm, Otto and I lay near each other with our noses practically in the dirt. We saw the wall of rain marching over the land. Suddenly water poured down on us. The fields immediately became oceans of mud. Water collected faster than it could run off or sink in. Lying on my belly in mud and water, I had to lift my head to breathe. A flood below and a storm above, where only calm sunshine had been moments before!

That is how Stalin's collectivization burst upon us. The roads suddenly gave birth to circling flocks of Russian soldiers. The stables filling the center of our long farmhouse quickly emptied. Horses, cows, pigs, chickens, geese, ducks, everything vanished into the communal center in the nearby village. Most animals later starved or froze in communal corrals from lack of proper care. Great famine followed the next year.

Then our workers deserted their quarters at the far end of our house, also to move to the communal center. We were Germans. We were not allowed. In fact, the men from most German kulak families nearby (including the husbands of Papa's many sisters) found themselves crowded into boxcars headed east. We never heard of them again.

We stayed all alone in our end of the house. When I crept into the empty regions of the building, smells of animals still lingered faintly in the air. Without them the stalls and wide center aisle seemed like a great hollow cave.

At the far end of the house the workers' quarters also had a stale, uninhabited smell. I tried to remember sounds, laughter and commotion, but a current of silence poured from the doorway. In earlier times I had felt drafts of warm air fragrant with cooking from that door. Inside, men drank tea holding lumps of sugar in their cheeks or ate from the great cooking pot using ornate wooden spoons they had carved. Seeing that huge room stripped bare, only dust drifting in the sunbeams, I realized just how empty our great house had become. Then they came for Papa, with autumn passing into winter.

Papa coughed and shifted in his seat. My thoughts returned to our train, to my family around me.

"Say, what is all that up ahead?" asked Otto, leaning across in front of me. "Buildings and such."

"It must be the outskirts of Kharkov," Papa replied. They were the first words I had heard from his lips in several hours.

Kharkov, at last! We rode all the way from the Black Sea to reach it.

"See if you can get to the German Consulate in Kharkov," Styopa told Papa one day in that prison. Styopa had worked as a hired hand on our farm. Then he became a party official in the new communal center. "You're still a German citizen," he said, very surprised himself. "I checked. Apparently neither your great grandfather nor anybody since bothered to change citizenship, so I can get you out of here. You go see what you can do."

Papa looked at Styopa silently.

"Listen, Friedrich, you were always fair and good to work for. But there's no place for you here anymore. This I can do for you, at least."

So Papa appeared late one afternoon, limping in from the road to our farmhouse. The shadows from the trees along the path fell across him one by one. We ran toward him, but for an instant no one could say anything. He broke the awkward silence by stepping up to mother and slowly, gently taking her in his arms. Then we were all upon him. He had so many bruises on his body, though, that our hugging and embraces were too much to bear. He had to break away after a moment, lines of pain creasing his face.

We followed him carefully into the house. He looked all around --into the barns, the empty stalls. He stepped into our rooms. No one said a word. We knew now we probably would be left alone and not shipped away in boxcars. But would our tiny store of food be enough? Even without him we had worried.

To soften the winter's hunger we knew was coming, Papa and Otto ranged over nearby fields every day. Once they brought the first ears of a whole cornfield they had discovered in the light snow as the weather worsened. Then as days and weeks passed, more and more snow fell. The sun rode low in the southern sky. Eventually the world became a frozen white desert. At times snow drifted right up over one side of the house, urged on by an icy, howling wind.

Defying the weather, Papa set off one day for Kharkov to pursue Styopa's suggestion. He had to pick a day when he could reach town and the train without being caught in a blizzard. With the winter sun shining bright and hard in the sky he struck off across the featureless landscape, leaving a long, faint trail of tracks in the snow. They remained for several days after he was gone. In the long dark nights, as wind howled and snow fell, I wrestled with my private fears. Was he trapped, freezing somewhere?

Eventually he returned, though. His trip hadn't resolved our situation but the German consulate in Kharkov would look into things over the winter. He planned to return in the Spring again, as soon as the weather was more civilized.

So we sat together around the great warm tiers of the ceramic hearth filling the center of our living quarters, and watched our food slowly disappear. The corn we had found vanished down to the last kernel. Mama even cooked the corn husks and we ate them, too. Sometimes as I sat listlessly, my stomach like an empty sack with the rat of hunger gnawing at it from inside, I thought with sad

Klara

amazement how completely the world can change. Only a year before the house had been bursting with food, the wealth of our farm a marvel to behold. Now we lived desperately from day to day, looking at a stewed husk from an ear of corn as if it were a choice feast. I still don't know how we got through that winter. Mama said God brought us through.

But Spring did come again at last, slowly and grudgingly. Papa set off for Kharkov. While he was gone small green buds appeared on the trees. In our anxious hunger we wandered about stripping off these little green morsels, taking them home to be made into soups. I still remember the pungent smell of nettle soup. It tasted like spinach. Hilda and Aline had begun to swell up from hunger, but gradually they began to run and play again and regained their rosy color.

Then one morning Papa returned, bearing new hope. His struggles during the winter had paid off! The German consulate declared we were indeed German citizens. If we wanted to go back to Germany, all we had to do was appear at the consulate door and they would take care of the rest.

Suddenly the house seemed to explode with frantic activity. The decision was made. We would leave right away, before anything could go wrong. We had the rest of that day to decide what to take with us. A great tension, a sense of urgency, filled the air. I tried to imagine leaving everything I knew, tried to say goodbye to all the things doomed to stay behind.

My silkworms were out of the question, of course. I didn't even try to plead about them. I knew it was absurd to think of carrying the great rolls of brown paper along in our flight. But I stood alone with them out in the dusty little room built onto the smokehouse, turning my gaze from the papers to the windows and back. In autumn before all the troubles, Papa would go to Mariupal to buy supplies like matches, kerosene, sugar, and a couple candies for each of us. It was on one of those trips that he returned with the silkworms for me. I was told not to open the brown paper until spring when the sun shone brightly and the mulberries were sprouting.

This summer the papers wouldn't be unrolled on the floor. Otto would not bring in branches thick with mulberry leaves when the little dots covering the papers came to life as hundreds and thousands of little wriggling worms. No one would watch them finish their feasting and spin themselves into the little cocoons which covered the stripped branches like some strange fruit. This year the cycle would be broken, and the little room would not witness the clouds of tiny moths emerge from the cocoons, fill the air with their fluttering, and litter the papers on the floor with another generation of eggs. No strong arms would carry the branches covered with cocoons out into the yard, plunge them into the huge cauldron of boiling water, and cook the silken husks off into a slimy mush. The drying racks, on which the disgusting slime was hung to dry, would not be opened. I would not take the dried fibers and spin them into the only raw silk to be found for miles around.

It had all been mine, my own project, my pride and joy. I would have no more silk for stockings or sweaters, or to barter with neighbors for items like apples, apricots, and pears. I don't think I shed any tears in that little room. When I finally forced myself to turn and walk away for the last time, though, the leaving left an empty feeling inside me.

By evening we seemed to be nearly ready to depart, though the sense of urgency grew stronger instead of fading away. The light of day faded into dusk. Darkness crept across the land, our land. We had gathered inside when Papa looked out the window and with a frown, strode quickly out the door. Someone apparently was outside.

A moment later he stepped back in and looked directly at me. Without a word, he motioned for me to come outside.

In the gathering darkness of the yard I saw a man's dark figure. After a moment I recognized my teacher, Comrade Plotsky. Surprised and alarmed, I stood close by Papa's side.

"Friedrich, I know you're leaving," he said. A shiver raced through me. How could he have known!?

"I had to come before you left. I wanted to say goodbye." Still my father said nothing. The stocky little man looked at me. "Klara, I must tell you I have taken a terrible risk for you. I should have reported you right away. But I knew if I did, you would be sent away to special schools, and you probably would hardly ever see your family again. I didn't want to do that."

Klara

I stared at him, frightened and confused. But I knew what he meant. I loved school desperately. I devoured my lessons as if they were a banquet. The thought of never sitting in that little school room again was even worse than abandoning my silkworms.

"I know it's best for you to take them all and leave," he said to Papa, as he took me in his arms and lifted me up to sit on the high rim of the great rain barrel standing beside the door. "But Friedrich, please promise me only one thing. All I ask is that when you get to Germany, send this girl to school. This is all I ask you."

Papa looked at me then. Still he didn't say anything, and his eyes were hard and serious. But I saw, too, that they glowed with pride. Pride in me! My heart beat wildly. I thought I would burst with joy! Then he turned away and the two of them walked out across the yard, talking softly. I sat on the barrel and waited for him to come back.

At last the next morning dawned. We were actually leaving, fleeing from the only home I had ever known. As soon as the sky began to lighten we gathered up our little bundles and stepped out into the morning air. A chill breeze and the grey half-light before dawn greeted us. Papa started off across the yard. We all trailed after him.

But almost before I knew what I was doing, I turned and ran back into the house. I looked around inside. Already it looked stark and uninhabited. Already ghosts and cobwebs were forming in the corners of my imagination. My family, everything that had made it my home, was outside and walking away down the road.

Papa came back in. He found me crumpled against the great hearth that sustained us with its warmth through the winter, a young girl of thirteen sobbing to herself. His mouth was closed and tight, his eyes were stern. But he was not angry. It must be terribly hard for him, too, I realized. Without a word, he took me firmly by the hand, pulled me to my feet, and led me out the door and across the dew-covered grass in front of the house. As we set out after the others as I wiped the tears from my eyes.

The sun rose higher. The day grew hot. We had been walking for hours on the dusty dirt roads, and I had grown quite tired when it happened. Figures appeared on the road ahead. We kept walking.

The figures grew larger, resolved themselves at last into the shapes of soldiers marching toward us. I saw Papa glance at Mama. No word was said. We kept walking.

The column marched in the middle of the road. We walked on one side. At first I thought they would pass us without a glance. But as the officer at the head of the line came even with my father, suddenly he held up his hand and the soldiers stopped. He had not yet looked at us. As he turned and walked toward us he took his pistol out of a holster strapped at his side. He only held it at his side, not bothering to point it at anyone.

"You are going somewhere?" he asked Papa. One or two of the soldiers behind him were holding their rifles, but most simply stood at ease looking across the fields.

Papa told him we were going to Mariupal to meet a train. He said nothing about going to Germany. No one would ever ask a single question if we all disappeared without a trace, I thought to myself.

Papa talked with the officer for several minutes. The man kept on the arrogant mask he had learned to use when dealing with civilians. Finally he decided to let us go on. As we passed the line of troops a few men glanced at us with a little curiosity, but most with eyes that hardly touched us.

Not long after this encounter with the soldiers, we got a ride on a farm wagon which took us right into Mariupal. We went straight to the railroad station to board the train for Kharkov. It was already standing in the station when we arrived, but we had plenty of time to clamber on board. We found our seats. While I gazed about me at our compartment, suddenly the train jerked into motion with a great roaring and clanking. My first train ride began by terrifying me. We were leaving the Ukraine and all the memories of my early childhood. They welled up inside of me as we pulled out of the station. First, I thought about Tina. Tina was a young girl who lived with us. Her mother had died in childbirth, and my grandmother took her in. Tina made butter which took all day long. Otto and I would run in hoping to sample and she would admonish us to go play, it wasn't ready! When it was finally finished Tina gave us tin cups of delicious buttermilk to drink.

Klara

Another memory came to mind. Great loads of manure had been hauled out of our stables and heaped into a small mountain behind the house. Styopa and Ivan appeared, pulling a huge steel drum by a long wooden handle. The manure roller! Barefoot, they rolled up their trousers to their knees so they could prance about in the manure and squish their toes in it. Otto and I joined in the fun. The pungent, earthy smell rose into the summer sky, accompanied by our laughter and shouting. I was appalled and delighted. After this rough treatment the great flat cake of manure lay in the sun for a long time, eventually fated to be cut up, stored away, and burned as bricks to keep us warm through the winter. Those manure bricks also escaped the great collectivization robbery. Who knows how we would have fared, hungry and alone, without the heat which they provided?

Now Styopa was a party official. He wore big boots and a long heavy coat. What did he really think of that? He had saved all of our lives and gotten us away from his "new order." In my heart he stands for the whole of Russia in those days. He was caught between the passionate, even heartless obsession with revolution, and the older and deeper bonds between people which seemed to grow right out of the rich black Ukrainian soil.

And so we came to Kharkov. A big open car with a German flag flying on the fender waited in the street outside the train station. Behind the wheel a chauffeur waved at Papa as we emerged onto the street. I climbed in with the rest of my family, a little uncertainly. He drove us down wide cobblestone avenues flanked by rows of tall and imposing buildings. Side streets opened to the left and right until I was hopelessly lost.

This brief tour ended suddenly in front of a large building, set back from the street. We had to look through a great iron gate in the stone wall around it to see it at all. Apparently this was the German consulate. The driver pointed and said something to my father. We all scrambled out.

I noticed soldiers guarding the gate, standing inside and looking at us. They wore uniforms quite different from the Red Army uniforms we had seen on so many Russian soldiers.

As Papa strode to the gate he pulled a sheaf of papers out of his shirt. He and the guards talked for a minute. One reached through and took the papers. His partner peered over his shoulder. They looked up again and began to talk with Papa, all in German. Their expressions grew more and more interested.

At length they handed the papers back through and opened the gate. One of them ushered all of us up the walk to the front door, while the other closed the gate again behind us.

"Welcome to Germany," declared our guide gruffly, as he opened the door for us. After we stepped inside he closed himself out. We heard the tread of his big black boots going back down the stone steps.

"I thought you said we were in Kharkov," challenged Otto. "Are we in Germany already?"

"This building is a little piece of Germany we've put right in the middle of Kharkov," a man's voice informed us.

We all looked around. He had come out of a room behind us and now stood regarding us thoughtfully. He wore shiny shoes, striped pants, and a wide tie with thin black and white stripes. He beckoned Papa through the open doorway in which he stood, and closed the door behind the two of them. They seemed to know each other. I could barely hear them talking behind it.

The rest of us were left standing in the wide central foyer, actually a hall running right through to another door at the back of the building. I had never seen anything like it. Even a simple thing like the white paint on the walls was new and striking. I felt out of place, strange. The air inside the consulate filled our nostrils with the smell of freshly sawn lumber. Several large crates stood about, tops off and half-filled with all sorts of things; lamps, vases, books and the like. We crept up and down the hall, peeking over the sides into them.

After a while, Papa stepped back out into the hall by himself.

"We didn't get here any too soon," he declared. "The consulate in Kharkov is closing soon. All the German diplomats here will be going home or to Moscow." We looked again at the crates, the meaning of their presence now clear to all. "In two weeks, or even perhaps only another one week, we would have come here only to find a boarded up building," he finished. Mama looked at him.

"In one more week?" she repeated. "I can't believe it! God has to be watching over us."

Klara

"Well, we've made it," replied my father. "We're going to get out safely and all of us together."

We would have to stay at the consulate for another day or two before taking another train for the final journey to Germany itself. Now that we actually had arrived, the final arrangements for our passage out of the country could go forward.

Carrying our little bundles, we crossed the highly polished hardwood floors and climbed the stairs. I gazed at the vast white walls, at the peculiar little ornaments set along them at intervals. We discovered what they were in our rooms, when Otto asked our guide about a switch on the wall. He told us it turned on the electric lights, demonstrating as he explained. We were struck dumb. The man left. Otto walked slowly to the light switch and turned on the lights. He turned them off again, and looked at me.

When Papa looked in on us Otto was still turning the lights on and off. Despite his fascination with this marvel of civilization, however, he had to stop it. We all had to wash up, Papa said. Soon some people would come around to our rooms with food. In the bathroom came my turn at discovery. What opulence! Each room had an entire bathroom of its own! Besides the running water for washing there was a commode. Above it on the wall hung a water tank for flushing. When Papa came again he found us flushing the toilet over and over. He made us stop that too.

The following days have run into a blur, but some memories of our stay remain clear. Otto put on earphones and listened to a radio broadcast on a crystal set. "It catches music out of the air," he said softly, only half believing it himself. We played records on a gramophone and listened to one of the German diplomats playing a piano. It was all amazing.

As if they were trying to outdo all these wonders, the junior staff arranged to take us on excursions through the rest of Kharkov. After breakfast one morning Papa brought in a young man, his blond hair flat and shiny, a tall collar stiff under his chin, wearing a striped tie and a black coat. He spoke both Russian and German. So did we, of course. Papa explained he would be taking Otto and me to see the Kharkov Zoo.

The open streetcars in the city then had wooden benches. On this particular morning they were jammed with people. We squeezed our little party onto one of them and went trundling through the streets. I glimpsed the city between people crowding all around me. It frightened and confused me a little, but I also felt a thrill of excitement. The city was a whole new world for me! Great brick and stone buildings stood shoulder to shoulder, surrounded by great walls with massive iron gates.

That day we saw animals unlike any we had known on the farm. I must have walked from one cage to the next gaping with wonder. Drawings in school books were one thing, but the real creatures, their smells, their noises, their living presence astonished and fascinated me. There were elephants, monkeys, bears, and all sorts of strange and wonderful birds. The idea of keeping such great barns full of animals just to look at them, though, took a little getting used to for farm children.

On our way out of the zoo we stopped at a little stand. The young man bought us the first maroschno (ice cream) we ever tasted. For days afterward, all the way across Russia, we talked about that ice cream. Riding back to the consulate, Otto quizzed our guide about just what it was; how it was made, and so on.

Another day, during a walk, we rounded a corner and I came face to face with a large bear. My heart jumped into my mouth! I stood frozen in terror, not even seeing at first that he was on a chain. An organ grinder stood beside him, though, chain securely in hand. Our guide persuaded the organ grinder to play, and the bear stood up fearsomely on his hind legs and danced for us. Otto was overjoyed but it scared me to death. I stood well to the back of the group, very glad when the bear finished and we started back for our rooms.

Then one very hot and sunny spring day our whole family clambered into the same large open car. The driver whisked us through the city and deposited us back at the train station again. It wasn't until then that I discovered our next destination.

"You better take this," said the driver, giving Mama a package that turned out to hold things to eat. "It can take a long time to get to Moscow."

Klara

Moscow! I hadn't realized we would go there. Why go to Moscow when we wanted to leave Russia instead? All roads led to Moscow, it was explained to me. At least, all railroads did. All the orders, all the soldiers, all the destruction of the last three years sprang from Moscow. I didn't think of that, though. To me Moscow conjured up a thousand images. It was a legend, the wellspring of Russia.

This train was not as nice as the one that brought us to Kharkov. The journey took several days and nights. We rode in large empty cars, without seats or compartments, and we slept curled up on the floor. The train was crowded with people. If we had not brought food in our bundles we would have gone hungry the whole trip. Each stop was a blessing for the fresh air it offered through opened doors, even when time was too short to get out.

When we finally climbed out of that train, crowds of people jostled us in the vast red brick square of the Moscow central station. Papa struggled against this human tide, looking for someone. He told us to wait while he went off in search of them. We huddled together and sat down with our bundles on the floor, as there were no seats anywhere.

The crowds swirling around us contained all manner of people; farmers, foreign travelers, city businessmen and party bureaucrats, other families. I was totally intimidated. I had never seen such crowds in my life. What would I do if I got lost in those crowds? But before I could worry further about it, Papa returned. He appeared suddenly, close by, followed by two men and a woman in Russian army uniforms. The men both wore fur caps with red stars on the front, but I was much more interested in the woman, the first woman soldier I had even seen. She also had a hat with a red star, and I could hardly take my eyes from it. What a hat!

The comrade soldiers guided us through the crowded railway station and got us on another open streetcar, which we rode through the streets of Moscow. I remember virtually nothing of where it was we went on that streetcar. The Soviet capital was just too big, too overpowering to make any sense. All I remember is that eventually we were shown into a very large room like a banquet hall, and told to wait. We weren't told what we were waiting for.

The room itself is my only vivid memory of Moscow. It was so huge that our family, gathered in one corner, hardly made any difference at all. It was still empty. And everything was red. The carpet was red. The immense, long curtains hanging at the sides of a whole row of tall windows were red velvet (though it wasn't until I saw velvet in stores in Germany that I found out what it was). There were indoor trees in great planters all around the room. Huge pictures of Lenin and Stalin looked out heroically from the walls. The chairs were red and black, and the general impression the room made was powerful and immediate. Red, intense red, shouted that here was one of the strongholds of communism. We were farmers in high places that day!

Then without warning, late in the day two men in dark suits stepped through the great double doors of our temporary refuge. Papa quickly walked over to them. After a whispered conference, he motioned Otto to come over. The four of them walked through the doors, Papa glancing back without a word at Mama. The heavy click of wood closing against metal cut off the low murmur of their voices.

Long minutes passed. We waited. I looked at Mama and I could tell she felt more and more nervous. The fear was contagious. What would happen to us without Papa and Otto? Was our luck, our escape, suddenly to end here in Moscow? I bit my lip and huddled closer to Mama. This terrible uncertainty hung thick in the air of the vast room for several hours.

Papa and Otto returned at last. Papa closed the doors behind himself. They had done something to him—there was blood on his fingers. Other than a short whisper to Mama, nothing more was said. Not until we crossed safely into Germany did I learn they had wanted to keep Otto behind, even though our papers clearly proved he was still a German citizen. He was not old enough for the army yet, but they wanted to keep him until he was 16, old enough to join. Papa told them, quietly and firmly, if they kept Otto we all would stay with him. They kept Otto alone for some hours, but finally sent him back to us.

A woman in a black and white uniform brought us food while we waited. We even spent a night there, sleeping in the big chairs or on the carpet. Early the following morning, though, it was back to the railroad station for us. Our exodus continued.

This time we had a compartment all to ourselves, with large padded seats and a wide window through which we watched the scenery. A dining car provided our meals. Beds for each of us opened out at night, and so we rolled across Russia to the west. Suddenly we were travelling in style!

The first morning Moscow passed before our window for a long time, and then open country outside the city with rivers winding among the big rounded hills. But before long we came into one of the vast forests which blanketed Russia in dark green from one horizon to the other.

"See," my father told me, "there are real Christmas trees!"

I'm sure that when he said that, we all immediately thought of the sort of Christmas trees he provided for us on the farm. In the dead of winter, shortly before Christmas, he would come into the house with a bare, frozen looking cherry tree over his shoulder. This little tree was watered and warmed inside the house, set by a window for light, and just about at Christmastime every year it suddenly bloomed in the middle of winter. Cherry blossoms littering the floor meant Christmas to me! I didn't like these giants in the fir forests as well as our little version of the Christmas tree.

We rode endlessly across Russia, looking at vast oceans of trees. At last we reached the Polish border. There we had to leave our train and walk across a space between two lines of track to board a Polish train for the trip across this new country. There was a brief discussion about our papers, and then we were in motion again across Poland. This trip took the remainder of that day and all of the following night, so we had to spend yet another night on the rails. The Polish train seemed less elaborate. We rode with a lot of other people in regular compartments. The free meals were over. My father stepped out a couple of times to bring us something to eat. We tried to sleep in our seats, not very successfully.

More than once during that trip across Poland I looked out at the lights of a town or village, wondering if it could be comrade Plotsky's home. I could almost picture his chubby face in the light reflecting from our darkened train window.

Actually, comrade Plotsky had been a signal of things to come if only we could have known it. One day in our little German school, organized for the children of the local community known as Prinzfeld, Herr Hoffenthal's lessons were interrupted suddenly. After a tremendous campaign on my part I had just started going to school with Otto. We watched Herr Hoffenthal's goatee bob up and down as he talked. As usual, one of the older boys had been whispering. He kneeled on a pile of stones for his sins.

Russian voices and the noise of a wagon filtered in from outside. Before we knew what was happening, Russian soldiers tramped in. Their great boots shook the boards in the floor. They wore heavy uniform coats and the inevitable red stars on their hats. Each man carried a rifle in his hands. They marched to the front of the room, past our silent, wide-eyed faces. Even the whispering stopped. They held conference with Herr Hoffenthal. He said nothing to them. They did all the talking. Then they escorted him out of the building, one of them vaguely pointing a rifle in his direction. It took only a few seconds in all. They were gone.

We children sat there alone, too shocked to lapse at once into noise as we otherwise would have done at the smallest chance. After a moment, almost as an afterthought, one of the soldiers came back in. He still carried his rifle. Would he shoot us? We had heard terrible stories. In Russian he told us to go home. School was over for the day.

Herr Hoffenthal and his family were put on a wagon that same afternoon. They were packed into a train in town, and that was the last we ever heard of my teacher and his family. For a few days after this stroke of lightning we had no school.

Then comrade Plotsky arrived. He was short and plump. He wore glasses, a hat and a double breasted suit like those worn in the cities at that time. From that day forward we learned our lessons in Russian, not in German. We learned about all the terrible evils loose in the world and how communism was struggling to cure them all. We never dreamed that all too soon we would come to be included among those evils ourselves. The number of Russian children sitting on our long wooden benches, writing with us at our long wooden tables, gradually increased. School definitely had changed.

Klara

As we rushed through Poland on the train in the darkness of a May night, I could not identify comrade Plotsky's home town. He never appeared magically on any little railway platform, waving and shouting that here was his home. I drifted into a short, entirely unsatisfactory sleep.

Early the next morning we arrived at Schneidemuhl, which at that time was the border crossing between Poland and Germany (today deep inside Poland as a result of postwar boundary shifts). Few people besides us left the train at the border, and those who did seemed to evaporate out of the station. By the time my father managed to extract a railway official from some hidden office we were alone in the building.

They knew vaguely we were supposed to be coming, but nobody believed it could happen. Certainly no precise dates had been announced. No one knew quite what to do with us. At last, after several very long telephone calls from the station manager's office, an old Red Cross car came and carried us toward our first experiences inside Germany.

For the time being we were sheltered in what may have been an old school building that had been abandoned. There didn't seem to be anyone in it except us. But we had a large room all to ourselves, with beds in it, and the bathroom down the hall even had a shower. Late in the day people started coming to see us. Nuns brought us soup. An official stopped in to have another look at our papers and to ask us about our plans. People from the German Red Cross were among the earliest arrivals. They brought us extra blankets, and arranged for Papa to come the next day and explore possibilities for us. Papa mentioned we were supposed to have relatives around Ulm somewhere, and they agreed to begin a search for them.

They seemed genuinely astonished by our arrival. It was unheard of for a whole family simply to be whisked out of Russia in those days of rising tensions, all in a group, all safe and sound. Once in a while some lone refugee managed to get out by crossing into Turkey or something, but our official transport and tolerant treatment were greatly wondered at. In fact, the next day photographers from Berlin newspapers came in to take our pictures. Everyone who came in developed a personal theory about why our whole family had been so politely escorted out of the country. One of the Red Cross people probably had the best explanation. We had appeared just as the Kharkov consulate was closing. We had wandered right into the middle of a sort of diplomatic spotlight. Once there, we had to be disposed of as an unpleasant accident, as quickly and with as much politeness and formal smiling as could be mustered on short notice.

I really cannot remember how long we stayed in that old school. The search for our German relatives was on, but such things could drag on indefinitely. Sometime later a Red Cross official came to talk to my father about an interim solution.

"Friedrich," he began, "as you know, we're still looking in Ulm for your family. We could find them tomorrow, or it might take as long as a year. Besides, when we do find them, there is of course a real chance they will not be able to offer much help to you."

"I don't really like to think of asking them for help, myself," commented my father.

"Of course not. What you really need is a job, a means of support, would you not agree?"

My father did agree. Much relieved, the man continued.

"We may be able to help you with this, then," he suggested. "We have found a possible job for you in a town called Melsungen. Unfortunately, it is quite far from Ulm, close to Kassel. Do you know where that is?"

We did not. As the Red Cross man described the little town to us, I saw a faraway look in Papa's eye. I imagined that he might be thinking back to the broad fields stretching away from our house, reaching westward over the plain from the banks of the Kalmus River. I tried to picture this little town crowded into a corner of our vast land holdings.

"You certainly won't be a large landowner any longer," commented our visitor, almost as though he were reading my thoughts. "I'm afraid this job will be a far cry from the sort of position you have enjoyed in the past."

"I certainly didn't expect to be a landowner again," Papa replied.

"Well," admitted the man, "this job is only working for the town as a groundskeeper in the public parks. It will be outdoor work." I suppose the thought of outdoor work in a park, pruning trees or raking leaves, must have seemed almost insulting to this thoroughly European civil servant. But my father had been a farmer after all, even though a pretty big one. I watched my father's face. His eyes never flickered. "That sounds much better than starving to death in a labor camp," he observed at once.

Since then I have realized more fully what a loss, what a drastic change this really must have been for him. But we never heard a word along these lines from his lips for the rest of his life. He was only passionately glad to be out of the camp in Starie Karan and out of Russia. His experiences in that prison had made him especially aware of the gift of simply being alive, though as a rule he would never talk about that place either. Just once I overheard him telling someone it was sobering what ordinary people could do when driven to extremes, eating anything in the desperation of starvation, even each other. But after saying that upon that occasion, he became very quiet and said no more.

"Then we'll telegraph the town officials in Melsungen and tell them to expect you! You will be able to go there in a few days. In the meantime, we will continue to work on your case."

Just as he promised, we boarded still another train only a few days later and watched Germany glide past the windows. I don't know what I expected to see. I think I really had expected Germany to look different from other landscapes, somehow. But of course all we saw was more of the great open northern European plain. We rolled across the green springtime landscape of the infant Third Reich, and it looked much like other landscapes I had seen from train windows. Since January, for about five months, Adolph Hitler had been in control of the German government. The Weimar era of liberal democracy was evaporating all around us, even as we rode into the country.

Of all this we knew nothing. We only knew we were all safely out of Russia together. I looked around at my parents, my brother and sisters with a little wonder. The scenery of our world seemed to shift and change beyond all my powers to keep up with it, and yet we still had each other. That had not changed, and it brought me a warm, reassuring feeling to look at all of them.

But there was more to it than that. I felt that somehow I had some special protection. A power greater than I could understand watched over us, kept us together, kept us safe. Now this power had lifted us completely out of my whole childhood world, but in my heart the sense of loss was balanced by a great relief and thankfulness. Sitting on that train, I recalled what my mother told me once about my earliest days of life. Not long after I was born in 1920, the battles between the Red Army and the forces trying to undo the Russian revolution swept over our part of the Ukraine. A band of Cossacks on horses descended upon us on the farm. This should have meant fire and sword, everyone dead and the place burned to the ground.

One horrible, wild fighter burst into the house. Mama stood there with me in her arms. Another of them came in. They looked down at me and gazed into my face. Then they turned without a word. The entire force of them rode away. No one was killed. When Mama described that to me, it seemed like she was describing a miracle from the Bible.

We found that the Melsungen train station rested part way up the shoulder of a low hill, above the town and the Fulda River flowing through it peacefully. Some town officials were on hand to meet us, and show us to an apartment already arranged for us. Apparently the whole town knew we were coming. In fact, some of the citizens had turned out to have a look at us. That first walk down the hill, across the footbridge, and into town was a strange experience. We must have been the smallest parade ever seen in that town. People stared at us as though we had just come down from the moon. Once or twice I heard people whisper. Once I caught the words, ". . . the Russian girls!"

When I heard those words, suddenly I felt very much like a big sister to little Hilda and Aline. I took one of their hands in each of mine as if to protect them, as we walked into town. Though I knew we were safe at last from the strangely metamorphosed Russians we had fled, I felt lonelier at that moment than I ever had before. I suddenly missed Russia very much. I wanted more than anything to be back in the farmhouse where I was born, with the animals, my silkworms, the dirt floors and warm summer sunshine. I could not understand why the entire great disturbance had happened. I heard familiar, comforting German spoken on every hand around me, but I had never felt so totally an outsider, a foreigner, in my life.

Chapter Two
YOUTH IN THE REICH

An old stone Lutheran church anchors the center of Melsungen. A low wall of the same gray stone encloses the churchyard. Built 700 years ago, it looks today just as it did in the Spring of 1933 when we saw it for the first time. Our new lodgings turned out to be in an old apartment house just down the street from the church. Timbered ribs of houses in this old part of town ran at crazy angles in the walls, with hardly ever a square corner. Many seemed as old as the church itself. Some were painted and clean. Others looked ready to collapse in the first breeze.

Our new house was three stories tall, crowded between neighboring houses much like itself. A dark, narrow hallway conducted us along the old brick floor, showing the wear of countless years of passing shoes. We climbed a narrow staircase, single file behind our guides. Sunlight filtered down through a small window at the head of the stairs. As we reached the top and stood crowded together in the hallway, one of our hosts pointed out the little white sink on the wall below the window.

"This building is equipped with running water," he announced. "There are pans and a pitcher in your apartment already, furnished by some of the people here in town." His partner opened a door on the left side of the hall, revealing an alcove with two more doors inside. One of these led into our two rooms, a kitchen and a living room. As we crowded inside awkwardly I suddenly recalled the bathroom attached to our room in the Kharkov consulate. But we had no running water at all on our farm, I reflected.

Our new surroundings did not seem very promising. We were by no means in the worst of it, though. Housing in Germany in those depression years was a catastrophe. In little farming villages some families lived upstairs with their chickens. The downstairs rooms served as a barn for cattle. In towns and cities poor households often crowded into one little room with their parents and perhaps some other relatives. Compared to these people our two rooms all to ourselves were more than adequate. The little town actually had done very well by us, considering the short notice the Red Cross gave them. After all, we were strangers from the fringes of Europe.

The welcoming committee wished us luck and departed. We rummaged about and inspected our new home. So now we were really living in Germany! Our long odyssey was behind us. Yet this new world was still a blank canvas beyond the walls of our apartment, as grey and impenetrable as the walls of the old stone church down the street.

One morning soon after we arrived, some of this new canvas was painted in for us. We awoke to Mama in the kitchen getting breakfast ready. We had to wake up, because the kitchen was where we slept. Papa's work in the parks of the town meant he left for work early. At first this left the rest of us on our own, but on this morning our idleness ended. In a house down the street lived a farmer of some means. My father had a long talk with him soon after we arrived. As a result on this morning Papa took all of us children with him when he left for work, and deposited us at Herr Grauer's door.

Herr Grauer was shorter than my father and quite stocky. From the start I was struck by the contrast between his pale freckled face and his dark red, rusty colored hair. He opened the door and stood above us. For Papa he had a hearty laugh and a neighborly handshake. For us he had a shrewd look in the corner of his eye as well as a smile. Papa told him what good workers we could be, and hugged us goodbye.

The Grauer children all had their father's shocking mass of red hair atop their heads, as I could see when his oldest son Heinz came rattling along the street, driving the farm wagon pulled by two big work horses. We all climbed on. In the Grauer fields outside the town the horses were unhitched and used for plowing. We were used for all sorts of things. We weeded tomatoes, cultivated potatoes, and fed chickens and pigs. At lunchtime we carried concentrated homemade raspberry juice out into the fields, to mix in big cans of water for the working men to drink. Otto sometimes worked with Heinz in the horse stables. They both looked young and strong, but already I could see Otto would be taller, slimmer, and more handsome.

Herr Grauer's shrewd glance had seen a good thing from the first. He got all that work out of "veteran" farm children, for the cost of our meals and sometimes some fresh produce for our table at home. My father's new career brought him only twenty marks a week for a family of six, though. Because our work left more of his wages for other things, out we went each morning that summer. The back of Heinz's head as he drove the wagon, red hair flaming in the early morning light, became a familiar sight. He and Otto became friends of a sort. Herr Grauer showed us his smile and treated us politely. His eyes looked past me when he spoke, though. We were useful to him. It didn't go beyond that. The Grauer farm was work on a smaller scale than our own farm, so even the hectic harvest time we took in stride.

I suppose this labor also was intended by our parents as a sort of preventive medicine. After all, it wasn't too long before everyone knew us as "those Russians." Paradoxically, we still were used to being "those Germans" from our time in Ukraine. Curious eyes followed us when we walked about the town to buy bread, meat, or vegetables. It seemed strange to be surrounded by Germans, safe from the Russians who had driven us out, and yet to feel alien and suspected anyway. We were still alone, but in a new and more complicated way. Good hard work would keep us from brooding over such matters and perhaps learning hostility toward our new homeland.

But finally our ability to cope with being foreign was tested by frontal assault. It was time to go to school. Our first summer had passed. We summoned up what little courage we could find and marched off to confront the real German children.

It was rough. The children were not reserved and polite like the adults. The provincialism and cruelty were direct and open. During the play period that very first day they began to congregate around me. They circled around me, staring silently. Then the taunting began. "Russky! Russky!" went up the chant.

This horrible treatment would have been quite enough all by itself. But the really crushing blow was not delivered by these German children. The school authorities decided to put me in with the little children in the lowest grade. My schooling in Russia counted not a jot. This was an infuriating, humiliating, senseless thing to do. After all, comrade Plotsky had done his job well. I could recite poetry, do mathematics, read and write both Russian and

German. Anybody should have been able to see I didn't belong in the beginning class.

Not long before our uprooting I even had won a special school prize, a chance to carry a huge red Soviet flag in the Mayday parade in Moscow celebrating the communist revolution. Streets were overflowing with people, soldiers in uniforms everywhere, and I had a uniform, too; a white blouse, a dark skirt, and a red scarf around my neck. We flag-bearers gathered in a great hall filled with the noisy confusion of students from districts far and near. We each carried heavy flagpoles. Huge red Soviet flags fluttered at the tops. The hammer and sickle in the corner of my flag seemed at least a meter across all by itself. Then we formed up into rows. When our time came we marched out into the already flowing current. The parade lasted most of the day. We marched and marched until I thought it would never end. All I saw, besides endless walls of faces along the sides of the street, were the forest of flagpoles and clouds of billowing red banners waving above our heads as we marched.

That night we slept on beds of straw spread on the floor of our assembly hall. The next day we returned home. That parade, a high water mark in my education, was also a sort of last flare of sunlight before darkness, though. Scarcely a year later our winter of troubles arrived and our world was shattered.

Now, from my glory carrying that great red Russian flag in the streets as a reward for excellence, I found myself reduced to an oversized dunce towering over the younger children. Why? It was explained to me that my handwriting was all wrong. In our German school in Prinzfeld the ancient, ornate German script had survived and was taught for handwriting. In Germany the times had changed. That old lettering was forgotten. Many could not even read it. I would have to start all over again, no matter what I knew. After that disastrous first day I walked by myself away from the town instead of going home. I walked out into the woods near the school, just outside the town, where I could look down on the roofs of the place I would have to learn to call home. I sat down among the trees alone. The tears came. It seemed that there was no room at all in this new world for me. No one would even let me or my family try to fit in, to become just another family in town.

Klara

Despite this stormy beginning, life gradually became more bearable. Several things helped brighten that first somber scene. The first was a visit on a Sunday morning. We were leaving for church when the sound of a motor car grew louder and louder. It stopped just in front of the house. Aline ran to the window where we all peered out at the town in the evenings. Hilda and I were beside her in an instant.

"There's people coming in here!" she shrieked excitedly. "A man and a lady!" We all crowded around but they had come into the building already.

"Somebody is getting company," remarked Otto.

We heard them come up the stairs. There was a moment's pause, then a knock on our door. We all stood frozen. I looked at Papa. His eyes met Mama's for a second. He walked to the door.

There stood a man who might have been Papa himself! Except for the high white collar and elegant clothes, that is. Their faces were as alike as I could imagine, though my father was a little taller, and more solid in appearance. Behind the man stood a tall woman, her pale features a sharp contrast to the severe black of her clothes. Their eyes darted over us quickly, sizing us up.

Finally the man smiled, and introduced himself as Papa's cousin Fritz from Stuttgart. We called him "uncle." There were candies for us children. Just as we had known vaguely about some relatives in Ulm and Stuttgart, they had known vaguely about some kin who had journeyed to the Ukraine in the remote and cloudy past. The German Red Cross methodically pursued this long lost link all through the summer, and the investigation had borne fruit.

Uncle Fritz was married with children of his own, but they had not come with him. By his side instead stood his sister Rosa, also from Stuttgart. Tante Rosa's dress was plain. Her hair was pulled back in a bun. She did not smile at us the way Uncle Fritz did. I discovered later she was very religious.

No doubt we got the visit off to a very good start simply because we had been on our way out the door to go to church. Rosa in particular seemed visibly relieved when she learned this. Perhaps she had been afraid we would be a band of Cossacks or something. We all went to church together, and with this formal start to the visit no one suffered through an awkward "greeting" period. After church many townspeople crowded around us, getting all the details straight about our family ties and so on. Herr Grauer and his wife made themselves very visible. With pride they told Uncle Fritz about how they had looked after us since our arrival. Finally we managed to break away and go back to our apartment for some lunch. Afterwards we children were banished from the house while the adults launched into intense conversation. All I heard of this was Tante Rosa asking, "...so how long did you say you have been living in this place?" and I was out. Children were to be neither seen nor heard.

We ran out to play in the street. Already the world was changing. Since people had been introduced to our real German relatives, we had somehow changed. The frosty distrust of the family of "Russkies" began to melt that afternoon. Uncle Fritz and Tante Rosa stayed nearly a week, though they spent nights in an inn. They seemed a little upset that Melsungen had deposited us in shoddy arrangements, though I still think the town did pretty well by us. When they drove away at the end of that week, we had taken a giant step toward acceptance.

Another key to adjusting for me was my teacher, Herr Gilfus. At my tender age he seemed the most distinguished man I had ever seen, with his neatly trimmed goatee, his pinz-nez and his cane. He taught the very young children in school but his interests went well beyond his daily round of work. He was intrigued by our family's arrival in Melsungen. He and his wife invited me to come and visit their home one evening. At first it was the story of our flight which they wanted to hear, but in succeeding days my teacher decided something about me.

"Klara," he said, "you have no business in my class. I think we'll have to develop some kind of special program for you. I don't like to see you wasting your time."

He gave me extra assignments. In less than a month, with his encouragement, I had finished the first year of school. Officially I stayed in his class, but I sat by myself in a corner of the room, working on my own. In the mornings I was the first child in the schoolyard. Every day I studied with grim determination. The sting of my shame at being placed with the smallest children never left

Klara

me. I loved school so much, and so much had been denied to me. Often I almost trembled with the fierce energy to succeed that possessed me that year.

The work of a second year fled past, and then a third as the winter passed out of 1933 and into 1934. That year was a race against time, though. While forced to start all over in secular education, I started the final year of religious training for confirmation. For most people my age, confirmation coincided with the end of grundschul (elementary school) and that was that. I would be confirmed along with everyone else, but what would happen to my regular schooling?

That confirmation class comforted and strengthened me, though, precisely because I was so far along. There I was accepted by other students my own age as an equal. In the last analysis, what mattered for acceptance were the rulings of adults. Through this class I finally began to make friends, and gain a feeling of belonging which I needed so desperately. The minister who led the class was also in league with Herr Gilfus in the plot to get me though school. Every time our meetings were over he took me aside to ask how things were going, and to offer encouragement.

Early in the Spring Herr Gilfus told me he thought we were working a little miracle. "Klara, this little project of ours makes me feel very good," he said once. "I enjoy my work, but I've never before felt this way. We are really accomplishing something unusual!" And he was right. I was almost caught up with the last grade. A month or two later, I was confirmed and completed elementary school at the same time. The minister gave me a bundle of books, including a hymnal, for a confirmation present. I still have the New Testament they gave me, and I will cherish it until I die. I took them home eagerly and read them over and over that summer. I had decided in my heart that someday I wanted to become a nurse.

The final thing which brought me closer to the other German children was quite different from all the others. I was recruited into the Girls' Hitler Youth.

I had been hoping it would happen, but it still came as a wonderful surprise when I was called to the school office. Along with all the other children in my class who were already members, I was finally being invited to join. Proud and relieved, I went to my first meeting that evening. I was presented in front of everyone and given my uniform. I didn't sleep at all that night, I was so excited. At last, that barrier to being accepted had fallen. I had taken another step toward belonging. We girls did all sorts of interesting things, like marching, songfests, picnics, hikes, and activity evenings. And it certainly was German! By belonging to it, so was I.

The other girls would stop at our house and pick me up on the way to meetings. I remember well how proud I was of my uniform. The skirt was navy blue. There was a white blouse, a brown scarf with a neckpiece, and a brown vest like suede. Together we would walk down the street, dressed all alike, laughing and talking gaily. It brought back memories of my communist parade uniform. I really belonged! The chants and taunts were gone. (At least, they were gone for me.) In fact, I urged my father to join the Nazi party so he could wear a uniform and march too. That never happened. At that time I never could understand it, because I thought he was such a good German. The combination of my Sovietized childhood and an uncritical young mind made it all seem very splendid and colorful. For that matter, plenty of older people seemed just as ready to accept national socialism.

In part no doubt this was because visible results of their programs came in rapid succession. First all the autobahns started to stretch across the landscape, linking cities and putting men back to work. Housing projects also appeared in many places.

And "appeared" is the word for it. Hitler didn't announce plans in advance. Rather, a project would be planned and carried out, and then Nazi propaganda pointed out these concrete accomplishments. Such a housing project appeared in Melsungen in early 1934. Since we had a large family we were eligible for one of the new houses there, if we could afford to buy it. The project was a sort of "suburb" across the Fulda River and up on the side of the hill above the train station.

Somehow, we could afford it! My father couldn't have saved the down payment, several hundred marks, despite the way we pinched pennies six ways. I guessed our relatives had given us some help in the matter, a loan or a gift. We moved in that fall.

No longer were we crowded into two little rooms. Now we had a kitchen, a bedroom for my parents, and a separate living room.

Klara

More bedrooms waited upstairs for us children, and we found plenty of room in the back yard to string a clothesline and plant a garden. A little stretch of green lawn in front ended at a picket fence around the yard, which we painted white. We were very happy. Such changes all around, like flowers suddenly blooming, perhaps helps explain in part why so many could tolerate the Nazis. In those early days we couldn't see what Germany was becoming. It only seemed to be coming alive again. There was a new sense of vitality and progress.

But "exceptions" to this prosperity were there to be seen, if only people had wanted to look. Down the street from us a little way, for example, lived a family with a daughter who had been retarded from birth. She lived in an institution in another city. Her fate gave a powerful hint of the darker side of the future in store for all of us. If only such incidents had been understood for what they were, and what they suggested as next steps!

For one day that family got a letter. Their daughter had died in her sleep. The letter was vague, unsatisfying, and final. It was all there was. This by itself would not have bothered my parents, but they heard of at least two other cases of other families in town, where the same thing happened within about a week.

"What does it mean, 'died in her sleep'? From what?" I heard her mother ask my mother. What could you say? We couldn't know it at first, but the cleansing had begun.

As months passed, other unsavory features of the Third Reich gradually crept out into the daylight. But always they seemed to occur at a distance from our own everyday lives. Events came to light as rumors, as isolated glimpses of strangers. The story of how the average Germans of that day were content to mind their own business is well enough known not to need retelling once more. There were six or seven incidents concerning Jewish families in Melsungen which I can recall. No doubt in fact there were more. One morning I heard Papa tell Mama all the Jews had been forced out of their homes, and their businesses had been taken away.

"Just like us Germans in Russia," she commented. Perhaps this feeling of what such persecution felt like from the receiving end acted as an inoculation against the anti-Jewish ugliness building up in those disturbing times. I know my parents didn't seem to share in the anti-Jewish fever. It was about then that I noticed my father seemed upset more and more often.

Then the time came for Otto, as the oldest, to leave home for a year of arbeitsdienst, required of every German youth under the new Nazi government. A vast pool of young energetic workers, they worked for free out of "patriotic spirit." This productive force certainly helped wake up the economy. Otto left home for adventures of his own.

Since I was out of school, it was time for me to begin my year of work service as well. Too small and light for farm work, I was sent as a household worker to the home of a local family named "Schiller" (not their true name). He was a prominent lawyer. Though he did not have a large family, somehow he was eligible to host pflichtjahr workers. The program was a good way to cultivate political support among powerful people.

The first day when I presented myself at their door, Frau Schiller met me herself and led me into the house. I judged her to be about thirty, rather thin but with a healthy, tanned face and red-blonde hair. She seemed unusually friendly toward me. They turned out to be a strange household, though. Herr Schiller took me aside one day to warn me.

"I don't want to alarm you, Klara," he said, "but the reason we are eligible for workers like you is that my wife has a very serious problem. Sometimes she is not capable of taking care of her family, so we need to have someone like you to look after the girls, to make sure they are properly fed and dressed and so on. We try not to say anything about it. If she should have one of her fits, just try to stay out of sight. It always passes."

Sometimes I did hear them fighting downstairs. He would usually leave the house when it happened. I would hear her roaming about downstairs then, shouting and crying, sometimes even throwing things in the kitchen. I sat frozen in my room. At last everything quieted down. During supper everyone would be was cheerful and polite again, as if the entire episode had never happened at all.

On such evenings, though, I couldn't help remembering the neighbor girl who "died in her sleep." For her retardation she most likely had been killed. Now here was another woman, also possibly disturbed. Instead of death, she got free domestic help courtesy of the Third Reich. This showed me the first serious flaw in my new homeland. Something was wrong, and power meant survival.

Advocate Schiller had two daughters in school, only a few years younger than me. Most of the time, my job was to entertain them and keep them out of their parents' way. They were charming girls, very pretty. They dressed well, got good marks in school, went swimming in the Fulda, took their piano lessons, and when we ran out of things to do I could always mesmerize them with tales about my life in Russia. The story they liked best was the harvesting of the sunflowers.

There on the shores of the Black Sea we had raised great fields of sunflowers, their golden heads towering high above the ground. At harvest time men rode down the rows in a wagon, one man standing on each side and one to drive. The two standing men swung long knives like machetes, chopping off the heads of the sunflower plants with single wide, clean strokes. Then they seized the head and pushed it back onto the stalk. There it sat, dead and drying while the stalk and leaves were still green. After drying for a time the same wagon would return and the heads would be seized once more and shaken into the bottom of the wagon, filling it with sunflower seeds to be carried away and milled for flour and sunflower oil. The girls had never seen such fields filled with tall sunflowers, marching in rows beyond the limits of sight. The image fascinated them, captured their imaginations.

Living near their house, I usually walked back and forth to work. In this way I managed to live at home even when I was supposed to be "away" giving my year to the fatherland. They had a huge house, though, considering it was in the middle of the town. There was a guest room upstairs, so I also stayed the night with them from time to time.

But in the midst of winter, near the end of 1934, my mother's childhood came back to haunt her. When she was only nine an epidemic had swept over her community in the Ukraine. It killed her parents and younger brother. Only she had been spared in the house.

Though her life had been spared, her eyes always troubled her. Now in Germany serious problems began. She took to lying down inside with a cool cloth on her eyes in the afternoons, but there was no way to halt the growing menace to her sight. Her eyelids grew swollen and inflamed. The doctor tried to treat them repeatedly. At last he said she would have to enter a hospital in Kassel nearby. So one day, Papa carried her bag and walked with her down the hill to the train station. He came back much later in the evening by himself.

This left me, the eldest daughter, responsible for the household. I kept house in my mother's absence and cooked the meals. My father went to the work bureau in town and got special permission for me to stay at home. My stay with the Schillers was mercifully cut short. I confess I felt a wonderful sense of relief the day I left that house for the last time.

As often as we could we rode the train to Kassel. There, in the outlying district of Wilhelmshohe, the great white walls of the hospital where my mother lay rose above the houses. The doctors told us only a long series of operations could save Mama's eyes. They confessed they were not sure what to do, but without their attempts she certainly would be blind and perhaps worse. Papa talked it over with her privately and came out to tell the doctors to go ahead and do whatever they could.

Whenever I went to see her, she always asked, "My child, is the laundry nice and white when you put it on the line?" That laundry was a sign to the neighbors of the quality of our home in general. Her question, repeated so often between us, made a deep impression on me. Washing fluttering clean and white on the line behind our house became a symbol of the direction my life was turning, as the fall turned into snowy winter.

The eye operations began. Over the next half year Mama had nine operations on one eye and four on the other. She stayed in the hospital all through the winter. Then as the spring of 1935 was beginning to give hints of its arrival, at last she came home to convalesce. We waited anxiously for several weeks, but then it became clear that the doctors had defeated her childhood legacy, at least temporarily. The pain would plague her all the rest of her days but the threat to her sight and health had been stopped.

Hitler's officials running the work bureau interpreted my interrupted year of service in the worst possible way, however.

Klara

"There are no four month jobs for special cases like this," Papa and I were told. "She simply will have to repeat the whole year with another family."

The words took a minute to sink in, but then they settled like a heavy weight on my heart. Instead of anger, all I could manage was a pitiable, resigned sadness. I felt beaten, trapped, and defeated. What could I do, except surrender another year of my life to these officials? And they didn't care a bit. They probably wouldn't even remember my name an hour after we left.

And so I found myself at the door of one of the highest ranking persons in town, Judge Kamm. It was autumn of 1935, meaning we had been in Germany for nearly two and a half years. At age 15 I had progressed no further than grade school, my own parents' kitchen, and a job as an unpaid servant. I knocked on the big door.

The four Kamm girls were younger than the Schiller children. The oldest was only nine. The Judge and his wife lived an incredible social life. At the peak of the local social pyramid, Frau Kamm's life was a whirl of parties, dinners, teas and outings. I shopped for groceries, helped the cleaning woman who came in every morning, and tried to be a substitute for the girls' parents. Frequently they packed up and left on holidays for a day, a week, or sometimes even longer, leaving me with the girls and the household.

It didn't take me long, though, to discover that I was in for a pleasant year. They lived up on a hillside, and the streets down into town grew dark and slippery once winter arrived. I lived there in their splendid house, though I sometimes managed to get home for a visit with my family on Sundays. I took the girls for walks around town and through the woods on warm fall afternoons, kicking through a carpet of new fallen leaves. These girls swam in the Fulda, too. As before, I had to be content to stand by the bank and watch. I never learned to swim. When winter arrived in force, we spent a lot of time sewing doll clothes. Still there was only fleeting contact with their parents. I read to the girls out of some books, read a great number of other books in that house myself, and the winter passed by very quickly.

Warm spring weather in 1936 brought visits to a country estate owned by friends of the judge. I rode along to watch the girls. Their house looked more like a castle than a farmhouse. Barns were barely visible as a set of red rooftops, thrusting their peaks above a nearby grove of trees. The girls had a wonderful weekend playing with the sheep and the dogs, making up names for the pigs, and running in the sunshine.

Shortly after that visit to the farm, Frau Kamm surprised me by telling me they would be sorry to see me leave. "We have a girl on pflichtjahr each year," she said. "But you take such an interest in the children! They really have come to love you; I think they will miss you terribly."

I thanked her for her kind words. I truly enjoyed my year with them, I said. I was glad to have been able to take advantage of all the new experiences their home had opened up for me. I really did like the girls as much as they liked me.

"We all will miss you," she repeated. "You know, I wish you could stay another year. Oh, I know." She must have detected the twinge of dismay these words created in me. "You've finished your national service. You want to go on to other things. I understand that, Klara." She smiled at me, and put her arm around my shoulder. "Well, we've enjoyed your stay. Please remember that, won't you?"

This was a touching little discussion, but my year of national service indeed was over at last! I said goodbye to the Kamms and went home once again.

My heart was still set on becoming a nurse. But I didn't have the schooling or the credentials. I didn't have any good connections that I knew about. I didn't have any money to live on while I studied. Some kind of job for a year or two seemed necessary before embarking on my career.

I had been keeping an alert eye on the B. Braun Catgut Fabrik, which manufactured sutures and other surgical supplies. If anyone in the world at large ever heard of Melsungen, it was probably because of this factory. The "better" girls worked there, the pay was above average, and the work was clean and not strenuous.

It took me some time to work up the courage I needed, but I finally decided to go through with it. I made my way down the hill to a little building beside the train station. A nervous knot of uncertainty tightened in my stomach. Job interviews belonged to Papa's world, the world of adults. Was I really ready to take such a step? There sat the Arbeitsamt, the work bureau staffed by the SA, Hitler's private political "army." This was the only way to apply for a job in those times. Such control of labor helped make business and industry friendly to the party, just as the year of national service made many friends among influential families.

An intense young man conducted my interview. I don't think he was from our town at all. I didn't know him, and a girl of sixteen would know the young men in her own town when it was the size of Melsungen.

Things started off all right. He smiled at me when I came in. I sat down in the chair set before his desk. He was about my age or perhaps a year or two older. I could tell he liked me. I had made a good first impression! That was important.

But the first impression didn't last. He looked down to the application form I had filled in at a table outside the office when I arrived.

"Born in Russia, eh?" he remarked with some distaste. I cringed inside, hoping my sudden dismay didn't show in my face.

"My family lived there for a long time, but they came from Germany originally," I replied. "We always spoke German at home."

He looked at me when I spoke, and then back down at the paper.

"Are you Jewish, then?" he wondered. "There are a lot of Jews in Russia, aren't there?"

I insisted I was just plain German, not Jewish. As we talked I realized he was struggling to find a category in which to place me. I watched, fascinated. It was a contest between his own native instinct to react to me as one individual to another, to like me and try to help me, and his Nazi training to judge everyone according to the rules of propaganda he had learned.

"What was it like to live in Russia?" he wanted to know. That question came from him, not from his training. My unusual background intrigued him, despite the fact that it made for awkward decisions in his job. I tried to tell him a little about my life. For a moment I thought the personal contact between us might triumph, and that as friends we might be able to talk freely and he would place me in a wonderful job.

We discussed my plans to study nursing. But somewhere along the way, I lost the battle in his eyes. I don't even know when I sensed it, but gradually the whole tone of the interview shifted. The propaganda won. He remembered the political side of his job. As we talked my heart sank. It almost seemed like a waste of time to go on, but we had to play the game out to its bitter end. Finally we got to the matter of a position in the suture factory.

"You want to work there? Well, I'm afraid that's just out of the question. Why, you're not even a real German! And you haven't been to any training schools, either. Not just anybody can walk in and get a job there. Why, with your education you should be glad to go scrub floors."

His attitude had come full circle. The decision was made. My category was settled. To overcome his initial friendly acceptance, it seemed he had to make himself deliberately harsh.

I was crushed.

Confused, despairing, I walked home feeling defeated and sorry for myself. It frightened and discouraged me to see how a perfectly nice fellow, who might have been a friend in another time and place, could force himself to such cruelty because he thought it was his job.

I sat at home feeling sorry for myself for many days. I had applied to several pre-nursing schools, where I could have boarded in and gotten the precious training he had complained about in my interview. I waited and waited, but not a word came from any of them. Then one day, while walking in the center of town, I chanced to meet Frau Kamm on the street.

"Hello, Klara!" she smiled. "How are you? What are you doing now?"

I had to confess I wasn't doing anything. All my plans had fallen through. She looked at me sadly for a moment. She was wearing a luxurious fur coat. I stared at it glumly, afraid to meet her gaze, but I did glance up in time to see a determined light come into her eye. Suddenly she took me by the arm and led me down the street.

"Come on, Klara. Let's step in here and have some lunch. I want to talk to you about something."

Now, I never stepped in anywhere to have lunch. That was one of those things I had no money to do. But we walked right into a nice little cafe, and she bought me a lovely lunch. We sat by the window looking out onto the street. I remember that in particular, because at one point during that lunch my friend Marta walked by the window and saw me sitting there, having lunch with the Judge's wife!

Marta and I sat together in confirmation class. She was probably my best friend in town. Walking by the cafe, she looked in casually and her eyes came to rest on me. That was a surprise! She looked again to make sure it actually was me. That was when she saw Frau Kamm. The sight of the Judge's wife chatting with me over lunch opened her mouth a little wider. I only smiled, not daring to disrupt our conversation enough to really acknowledge her surprise, but later we had a long talk about that lunch!

Frau Kamm wanted me to think again about coming to stay with them for a second year. They had not yet decided on a new girl, she explained. If I only would come for one more year they would gladly pay me a small salary, though they could get someone else free on national service. The children often asked about me and missed me very much.

I told her I needed to think about that. She was very gracious. We finished lunch, and I walked home slowly, thoughtfully.

I talked it over with my parents later that day. There really wasn't much to talk about, though. What other alternatives were open to me? The next day I walked to the Kamm house and told them I would come back for another year.

This time I was paid some tiny wages, which I had little use for since my time was quite filled up with my work. I turned most of this money over to my parents. The girls were overjoyed to have me back again. I was happy to see them, too.

But the small salary and my enjoyment of the girls was nothing compared to my great disappointment. That first day back in the Kamm household I stood alone at the large window in the sitting room, surrounded by elegant furniture, looking down on the town from a home that was not my own. None of it was really mine. My own dreams seemed to be getting nowhere. I seemed destined to live in a backward world of household drudgery and petty jobs. At times like that, when I might have felt bitter, I found myself thinking back to Russia instead. What had happened to all my little cousins? To my wonderful aunts? When I thought about them even my worst disappointments didn't seem so bad. I felt sure, somehow, that I would be lifted up again and that my life would come out right.

Klara

Chapter Three
BLOSSOMS OF SPRING

Whether making beds, washing dishes, or playing "five stones" (a Russian game, a little like jacks) with the Kamm girls, what really kept me alive during that second year with them was hope. If only I could go back to school! If only somehow I could find a way to make my dreams of being a nurse come true! That hope animated me as the year went on.

Judge Kamm was tall, lean, with silver hair. Perhaps it was only a habit he developed on the bench, but he always seemed calm, his thoughts reasonable. It was as though he listened to every conversation, every remark, as if it were a legal argument to be considered. I respected him tremendously. I also thought of him as a kindred spirit, someone who would understand my own heart, for he also seemed to love knowledge. He always dragged home books, piles and piles of them. I wished he would bring home books about nursing! I couldn't really get to know him personally, though. He could hardly become friendly and chatty with a young girl working in his household.

On the other hand, I did get to be something like friends with his wife. Frau Kamm impressed me, too, from the first day I met her. She wasn't from Melsungen originally. The Judge was a local boy in his youth; in fact they lived in the house where he had grown up, used to the best all his life. She met him in Munich during his university days. When he came back home, she came with him. At least from outward signs, she seemed to have found her place in local society. She seemed happy.

She was from Bavaria, but certainly wasn't a "bauern from Bayern," a rustic, husky farm girl. Tall like her husband, even statuesque, she looked several years younger than he did. Mahogany tones in her hair framed the smooth, sharply-chiseled features of her face. This natural beauty always enjoyed the luxury of cosmetics expertly applied. Until I lived in her house I never understood just how much time and labor fashion demanded.

Sometime that autumn she began to ask me to help her with her hair. At first I only handed her a towel or things like that. But before long I stood behind her, brushing her hair out and regarding the pair of us in her wide dressing table mirror. I admired the gilt-edged mirror. I admired her silken dressing gown. I admired everything, even the hair brushes. At rare intervals I even dared to slip into that dressing room alone, and regard myself in the mirror. Would I ever live like this? Though it seemed unlikely, I dared to dream of it.

Around this time, boys started to pay more attention to me, especially Heinz Grauer. From what I could gather, Heinz took an "I-saw-her-first" interest in me. It might have started with those morning wagon rides out into the fields. He had grown since then. His hair was still bright red, though. I couldn't help it but when I looked at him, I saw the beginnings of a "farmer" as that species appeared to people like the Judge and his wife. I told Marta I certainly wasn't interested in him. It can be very helpful to have an older brother, too. Otto could see our peers from an entirely different angle. He had gotten to know most of them as friends before he left on his year of Arbeitsdienst. Once when he came home from his travels he had a little chat with me.

"Do you know Heinz Grauer talks about you all the time?" he asked me.

"That's what Marta told me. But he never says anything to me."

"Well, what do you think of him?"

"I don't know, Otto." I didn't say he seemed crude and dull. "I don't know him really, except from the work we all did that first summer. You remember."

"Well, I thought I'd better tell you about him," Otto replied awkwardly. I could see he felt self-conscious playing the big brother. "You know that Heinz drinks too much." I hadn't known any such details. "Actually, he likes to be drunk. Did you know he already hit a girl once while he was drunk?" This idea shocked me. I knew it happened, of course, but to someone our age? A boy I knew personally? "You don't need that kind of treatment," my brother declared seriously. "You ought to stay away from him."

The prospect of getting involved with someone who at nineteen already was getting drunk and slapping girls around was ugly and frightening. I was glad my brother was around. Of course, it didn't hurt that he also relayed other choice pieces of information. One evening at dinner, for instance, he created plenty of blushes and smiles. He announced the butcher had told him that his sisters had the best looking legs in town. Papa looked amused. Just a stray comment, of course, yet I still remember it. It did me no harm to hear such news.

My main responsibility continued to be the girls. Sometimes I felt like I was becoming their mother. They always came to me with problems. Sometimes, I think, they too saw me as their mother.

Then came a clear, sunny spring morning in 1937. I had just come back from another of the weekends in the country. I was sitting in the drawing room. The children were gone off somewhere. Frau Kamm came in and sat down close beside me, looking as regal as ever.

Sisters Klara, Aline and Hilda

"Klara, I know you often talk about wanting to be a nurse. You once applied to several places for preparatory training, didn't you?" I nodded, not knowing how to react. "Did you ever hear anything from any of those places?"

I told her none of them had ever sent me a single word. She only nodded her head. But she came back to me one day not long after our discussion, all business. She brought me an application form for work at the sanatorium above the town, crowning the ridge along one side of the Fulda River valley. In fact, she mentioned she could easily get applications from any of several such training programs in nearby towns. I could have my pick of them, it seemed!

Why was she doing all this for me? The first day I met her, two years earlier, she had seemed so lofty and aristocratic I knew I could never be anything but an insignificant detail in her life. She had her own children to consume her kindnesses, after all. Yet she took an interest in me, bought me a lunch, paid me a salary, and talked to me about my future. She was a remarkable woman. I think I had grown to love Frau Kamm.

"It's only a pre-nursing preparatory program," she explained. "It's not really nurses' training. But it is important to have experience like this when you apply to a training program, since you have no other schooling except Grundschul."

Judge Kamm wrote a letter recommending me. I sent in the application. And as smoothly as that, I was accepted!

I showed Frau Kamm my acceptance when it came. She only smiled, finished a line of the letter she was writing, and then gave me a hug. She and her husband were pleased but not really surprised. In their position, I suppose, they usually got what they asked for. My parents were pleased and shocked, and they came to think very highly indeed of the Judge and his wife. I just had never realized they could be "contacts" in this way. The idea had never occurred to me in the two years I had been there.

I was on top of the world, walking on air the whole summer. I left the Kamm household and waited impatiently for my new life to begin. My dream was coming true, when only a year before my life had seemed a blank wall of despair and dead end jobs.

Marta Kiel shared that summer with me. We grew into closest friends. She too was waiting to study at the sanatorium. Our lives seemed to be on parallel tracks: both seventeen years old, both swept up in the experience of blossoming into young women. We were even about the same height. We could wear each other's clothes. We had been together in confirmation class, then in the girls' Hitler Youth, and now we would work together. We spent many warm sunny afternoons speculating about what was in store for us. Marta's father supervised the heating plant for the sanatorium where we were waiting to go to work. The Kiels had a little house on the grounds, just down the hill from the main building. Most of her life actually had revolved around that hospital.

Marta came from a deeply religious family. She dressed in very plain clothes. She and her family went to church constantly. They let her have almost nothing to do with boys. She came to terms with this personal world by immersing herself in her study of nutrition. She was quiet and serious while I tended to talk and laugh a lot. Still, we found a bond growing between us, a warm friendship that became very important to us both.

Then at last autumn arrived. From the very beginning that time seemed dreamlike. Days were full of bright colors, leaves drifting down around me as I walked up the hill with the warm morning sunshine in my face. That morning walk quickly became precious to me. I could feel, perhaps, I was going somewhere. Not just up the hill, but toward a new future. Those morning walks made me happy, and at peace with myself.

We were not studying exactly the same thing, since she aimed to be a nutritionist instead of a nurse like me. But both Marta and I spent two hours each afternoon in classes, after working all morning at the sanatorium. I was back in school! Every day I rejoiced to myself over my good fortune. I savored my lessons like a special dessert.

Sometimes Marta and I ate lunch together in the cafeteria, or walked across the lawn to her house. Sometimes instead of walking down the hill in the evening I would spend the night with her. Then we could lie awake together in the darkness dreaming of our futures. We were full of great plans that winter.

Cold months rushed swiftly past, muffled in thick snow. Along with my everyday chores I gradually began learning some of the duties of the sisters working as nurses. I call them sisters, but it was not a Catholic hospital. They were Lutherans like me, an order of nurses specially trained and supported by the church. They were actually "deaconesses," but everyone called them sisters, even they themselves. Most of the people with whom I worked were sisters.

Sister Konstanza was in charge of the second floor wing where I worked. I tried to keep out of her way. Perhaps a little over fifty years old, certainly she was old enough to be my mother. But she was very much bigger than my mother. She was a whole head taller than me. Despite my caution I often encountered her in the hallways, and I'm afraid I must have cringed a little from her big, angular form. She seemed so stern! Her patients, her order, and her career seemed to sum up her life. She had never married. Instead of children of her own she had us in the preparatory program, and she treated us as if we were her children.

"You'd better watch out," I would tease Marta over lunch. "I saw the way you and that new corporal were looking at each other. Sister Konstanza will catch you!" I was not alone in feeling intimidated in her large, stern presence.

"It's perfectly proper, Klara; we were secretly married two days ago!" We would break into laughter. Most of the patients were soldiers. Many were quite young and handsome. But any personal relationships between patients and staff were strictly, rigidly forbidden. If some dapper young soldier got funny ideas, the girl would be packed out the door instantly and permanently.

Warmer spring weather once again tentatively asserted itself. It was 1938. In April I turned eighteen. The Kiel family had a little birthday party for me. My parents and sisters came up for the occasion, but Otto was gone in the army, as always.

With warm weather, we began taking patients out for wheelchair rides in the morning air, and I could glide along slowly, rolling my charge before me. My thoughts drifted up away from the green hospital lawns, to float across clear spring skies.

As I went about my routine, I found a deep sense of satisfaction growing within me. The classes, the preparatory work was nearly finished. My marks were high. I was making it! How little I suspected what was about to happen.

While carrying trays out into the cafeteria one day, I noticed one of the patients gazing at me intently. A tremor of anxiety flashed through me. It could mean trouble, if he was getting funny ideas. I considered what to do. I should move calmly, capably back into the kitchen and stay there. Find something else to do until lunch was over. I started for the kitchen.

But my path led right past his table. A circuit out of his way would let him know I was reacting to his glances. He was still gazing at me.

I fixed my eyes on the kitchen door and my mind on looking business-like, unaware of this handsome fellow, even as I passed within arm's reach of his chair. Within arm's reach? Suddenly and quietly, his arm reached out. I felt his hand press something into the apron pocket of my blue and white striped uniform.

Klara

Impossible! I almost jumped away from his touch. Instead, I managed to glance at him. Casually, calmly, I finished my walk into the kitchen. The kitchen door swung closed behind me. I moved a little to one side, out of the path of other people, and stood very still for a moment.

The moment our eyes had met etched itself in my memory in uncanny detail. His face was turned away slightly, deliberately. His pale grey eyes sparkled. How do you explain that feeling of knowing? Usually people merely see each other. This time I felt a current suddenly flow between our eyes, charged with meaning. His eyes spoke to me, but I didn't look long enough to find out what they were saying.

It was startling to discover all this in an instant in the eyes of a young soldier ill with tuberculosis. Working in the hospital we knew the disease was notorious for stimulating such feelings in its victims, but somehow I could not simply chalk up the incident to that source.

I stood still a bit longer, trying to reduce that instant to manageable size. Gradually my heart slowed its pounding. My senses cleared a little. I could look around again, recognizing faces and walls around me. Before I could stop myself, my hand darted into the apron pocket and discovered a folded square of paper. The note!

I walked straight into the washroom. There, fearing at every breath to be interrupted and knowing I could easily find a more private place, I took out the note and unfolded it.

"I don't want to cause you any trouble," the writing said, "but I would like to meet you. I will be in the radio room this afternoon. Will you meet me there?"

The radio room? I put the note back in my pocket. The radio room was a patients' lounge, at the opposite end of our wing from the central staircase that led down to the first floor. A large, expensive console radio had been installed there. People came out of their rooms to enjoy the sunshine that poured in through a wall of south facing windows, and listen to the broadcasts.

Would I meet him there?

I walked back out into the kitchen. Washing dishes after the completed midday meal provided a welcome task for my hands, while my mind bounded furiously around the hospital, always ending at the radio room and a feeling of blank confusion.

In the end I resolved to walk past the radio room and just glance in as I went by. Perhaps he wouldn't even be there. I took a tray with a full water pitcher, and walked through the halls to the radio room.

He was there. I saw him sitting on the simple cloth couch, bathed in a flood of afternoon sunshine. My heart was pounding in my chest, so fast I thought it might flutter right out and fly away. I carried the water pitcher over to a table where its empty cousin sat. As soon as he saw me in the room, he got to his feet and walked over to stand beside me.

"I'm glad to see you," he said, taking one of the empty glasses on the table. I poured from the full pitcher for him. When I found myself again looking into his eyes, I knew I wasn't going to just walk out again. His voice sounded wonderful. I drew a deep breath and let it out again in a sigh to try to relax. My heart was still pounding nervously. I didn't trust myself to open my mouth and not say something foolish. I held up the note and gave him a questioning look.

"Oh, I know that was a crazy thing to do," he said earnestly. "Really, I don't want to make you any trouble. I just couldn't think of any other way to get a chance to talk to you. Do you know I've been watching you for four days now, ever since I got here?" I must have looked a little surprised at this. He continued, "Yes! Each day I wanted more and more to meet you, to talk to you. Can you tell me your name?" He looked at me, no hint of hesitation or pretense about him at all. He seemed oblivious to everything but the two of us. I felt myself drawn into this intensely private mood. It was an extraordinary feeling.

"I'm Klara," I replied. I extended the note to him. "You'd better take this back. I shouldn't have any incriminating evidence in my pockets."

He gave a little laugh and took the note. "Klara." He said my name, just once. "It suits you. I like you even better now that I know your name." I blushed and glanced away out the window for a moment. His voice brought my eyes back.

"My name is Rudi. I imagine you know why I'm here." I nodded and smiled, so he went on. "I was drafted into the army nearly a year ago, but even then my health wasn't good. I only went into the reserves. Then they found out it was tuberculosis. My parents got me sent here."

As we stood together in the sun I suddenly wondered what strange new world I had stumbled into. At last I told him I had to get back to work. It seemed we had been standing together for hours. Actually, it had been a couple of minutes. I put the empty pitcher on my tray. Rudi walked me to the door.

"When can we talk again?" he whispered as we reached the hallway. I turned to him, unsure of what to say. "Come back again tomorrow?" he suggested. "Please, Klara?" I looked deep into those grey eyes. There was no way to respond except to nod my head.

He broke into his wide smile. "Good! See you tomorrow, then!" he whispered emphatically. As I turned to go, he stepped after me into the hall. "Klara," he repeated, taking my arm in his hand as I turned back, "I've been in love with you since the first moment I ever saw you."

Abruptly then, he released my arm and walked quickly back into the radio room. For a second or two I stood there in the hallway, my head still whirling, I managed to walk away down the hallway. In one brief half hour my world had been turned on its head.

I did go back the next day, and the day after. I was in love with him, too. I dreamed of him sometimes at night. My days revolved around our short rendezvous each afternoon.

"I can't seem to remember what the world looked like before I met you," he told me. "I don't see things as I used to. You've changed me."

I hesitated. "I feel as if we are living in a fairy tale," I replied quietly.

He didn't think it sounded foolish at all. From the first, we realized that there was indeed a dreamlike quality to our days together.

As our conversations went on I told him my plans to become a nurse, and discovered that he dreamed of becoming a surgeon. He came from an important, even aristocratic family. His father was the mayor of Mainz, one of the oldest medieval cities in Europe, a historic seat of German culture.

"Your lover is very handsome," commented Marta Kiel a week or two later. It was like being awakened in the middle of the night by a loud noise.

"What did you say?"

"I said," she smiled quietly, "your lover is very handsome. A couple of girls on the staff are jealous of you. You're lucky, Klara."

I must have blanched as white as new snow. I was horrified. Everybody knew about our secret romance! It could only be a matter of time until I was thrown out of the hospital. I was ruined!

Marta laughed at my despair.

"Oh, Klara, don't look so pale! No harm will come of it."

I couldn't believe that.

"Do you think this has never happened before?" she asked. I had to stop and think about that. I never heard about someone actually having been turned out for a hospital romance. I suppose I had naively assumed such romances just never happened. On examination that couldn't be true. A flicker of hope returned.

"How long have you known, you wicked girl?" I demanded.

"Oh, I saw you in the radio room a couple of days ago, giving each other those long lingering looks. But that was only after Bertha told me about it."

The whole hospital staff crowded into the hallway outside the radio room, pushing each other for a chance to peek in at Rudi and me murmuring to each other? I felt foolish, and still more than a little frightened.

But Marta was right. I got proof only a couple of days later. I came trundling a wheelchair down the hall one morning to pick up Herr Drexler for his turn in the fresh air. Sister Konstanza emerged suddenly from a room as I passed.

"Good morning, Klara," she said.

"Good morning, Sister Konstanza."

"All set for a constitutional, I see. Klara, I think we'll have someone else take Herr Drexler out today." She stepped closer and lowered her voice. "Why don't you take Herr Leutner for a ride this time?"

That was Rudi! She was instructing me to take Rudi for a wheelchair ride around the grounds! What did she know? I looked quickly into her eyes. To my unbounded astonishment, Sister Konstanza winked at me! There was no mistaking it. It was my second revelation in less than a week. Inside that tall, spare frame there beat a heart full of soft romance, a heart tuned to love stories and moonlit strolls, to soft music and whispered endearments. Sister Konstanza! Without that undeniable wink and her happy conspiratorial smile, no one could have convinced me that such a thing was even remotely possible. But it was true. What a lot I still had to learn about the people I saw around me every day. She walked away, humming a little tune to herself.

And that is how it came to pass. Rudi and I took our daily journeys, he in a wheelchair, blanket on his lap, me in my blue and white uniform pushing him along. From this airy plateau of strolls on the lawn we watched our surroundings almost like the set of a play in the theatre. The world seemed always at a distance, as though we had entered a small space in our lives set apart from all that had come before, and all that was to follow. Wherever it was that we had entered, it was a place reserved for just the two of us.

What did the future hold for Rudi and me?

The next day I took him for our walk around the grounds. He was sitting in the wheelchair as we glided along, telling me about growing up in Mainz. I was looking down absently at his wavy brown hair, unable to see his face. Finally we rolled back to the hospital. Lunchtime was approaching, and after that I had my classes.

That evening I decided to tell Mama how I felt about Rudi, and possible future together. To my astonishment, as soon as I mentioned Rudi she told me some news of her own.

"Rudi was here this afternoon," she announced. I was too stunned to say anything, so she went on. "A car from the hospital stopped outside the house here. He told me it comes down every day for supplies and mail, and he just got a ride in it. He was wearing his uniform. He looked very impressive. All the neighbors were staring out their windows."

She smiled at the memory. Mama didn't smile very often. It made me feel good to see it. She went on. "He told me all about it. He says he loves you, Klara. He wants to marry you." He hadn't actually asked me in so many words, but I knew that. He had already talked to me about this possibility.

"I have a letter to show you," he had said unexpectedly one day, not long before. It was to his parents in Mainz. In it he told them all about me, and I hardly dared to believe that it was me he was writing about. He wanted to bring me with him and come home for a visit. He told them he wanted to marry me.

He mailed his letter, and our future seemed secure. Every day was warm and sunny. Everyone around us seemed tailor-made for our own happiness. The world was almost perfect.

But tuberculosis is an uncooperative disease. It refused to recognize true love. Rudi's cough slowly grew worse. Sometimes I would sit on his bed helplessly, watching him cough for minutes at a time, barely able to catch his breath between fits. He would glance at me, pain mingled with an amused look of resignation in his eyes. Then I felt my helplessness doubled. Still, the fits always passed and the clouds parted to let our sunshine return.

Rudi got a reply from his parents. They were distinctly cool about me. He showed me the letter.

"You're not Catholic!" he exclaimed, exasperated. He and his family were Catholic. He wrote back the same day, telling them we could all talk about it when he and I came home together at Christmas. This was no last word, though. Not long after that he got an even more negative letter.

"If only they could meet you!" he said. "I know all this nonsense could be cleared up!" But we had to keep such animated conversations to a minimum. The slightest exertion could bring on an agonizing spell of coughing. It tore at my heart to have to sit and watch him helplessly as the disease had its way with him.

Then one day he coughed up a couple of little flecks of blood. They flew from his mouth and landed on the clean, white sheet. There they were, tiny red specks, insignificant and terrifying. It took a moment for me to react, but then I was seized with fear. I got Sister Konstanza, who got two of the doctors.

"This cannot go on, Rudi," one of them said. "You'll die unless something is done."

"What will you do?" he asked.

"We cannot do what needs to be done here. I'm going to contact your parents and have you moved to Davos, in Switzerland. They can help you there, I'm quite sure."

Rudi looked past the doctor straight at me, as this sudden news sank in. For the first time I saw fear in his eyes, a look I could not understand.

When we were alone later I tried to put a cheerful face on it.

"So you're going for a vacation in Switzerland!"

He didn't respond right away. "I wonder how long it will be before we are separated?" he said, half to himself. It was not long. In fact, it must have been only a few days before he told me his parents were coming the following morning. They had called. They would take him out of the hospital and drive him to Davos themselves.

Once they arrived, I met with Rudi's mother the afternoon before he was to leave. We had coffee and cookies. She said that Rudi still had two years of medical school. She also said that I would never be accepted into the family. I was not Catholic, and even if I converted it did not matter to them. That was the end of our meeting, and I knew I would never be able to join his family.

Later that night I sat with Rudi for the last time. It was the only time I ever saw him actually cry. "I can't bear this, Klara," he said to me. "I promise, I'll write to you every day."

"Oh, that's crazy. You can't write every day," I said. But he insisted that he would write to me as often as he could. He begged me to be sure to write to him.

"I'll recover faster than anyone believes possible!" he declared. "I'll make medical history! And I'll come back and get you when I do, Klara."

We sat together for what seemed like forever in his room, holding each other tightly and saying very little. It couldn't have been too long, though. Eventually I stood up to go. My cheeks were stained with the tracks of tears. I washed my face in the basin of water in his room.

"I'd better go, Rudi," I whispered. "I think it will be easier for us if I'm not around when you leave."

We shared one last desperate close embrace. Then I fled out of his room, to the far reaches of the hospital. For a little while I roamed about the building, my heart full of despair, longing to be with him again, even for just a few last minutes. But I fought down the urge to run back to his room. It would be all wrong, and I knew it. We had taken our leaves for the present.

I made my way to the kitchen and kept busy breaking eggs for breakfast. Broken eggs, broken heart, I thought, and then had to smile at the melodramatic sound of that. I filled a couple of large pitchers with broken eggs and added salt and milk to the mixture. Perhaps they were already in his room gathering up his things. Again the urge to run to him; again I fought it down. After breakfast I sought for something else to do. At last I seized a wheelchair and rolled it to Herr Drexler's room.

"Klara!" he exclaimed, "I'm so glad to see you! Where have you been these last weeks? I thought you had left the hospital!" A sweet old man. I helped him into the chair. "I've missed our little talks," he told me, as we rolled down the hallway and out the door onto the lawn. "How is your brother in the army? Have you heard from him?" We made our way across the lawns to the trees. I turned the wheelchair to go back.

There they were. A large grey car, open top folded back, stood in front of the main entrance to the hospital. A tall white-haired man and a woman wrapped in furs helped Rudi carry his bags down the steps. The driver was opening the luggage compartment. Even as I got the wheelchair turned about and pointed back toward the building, they stowed the last bag and climbed into the car. I stood rooted to the lawn. Herr Drexler didn't even seem to notice we were stopped a fairly long time. I didn't move again until the car started up, and with an unspeakably strong air of finality, drove away down the hill through the gate.

I felt completely hollow inside. I hadn't heard a word Herr Drexler had said for perhaps a minute or two. Suddenly the world, so

Klara

full of life and color only a day ago, an hour ago, seemed painted in shades of grey.

Eventually I strained against the wheelchair to set it moving, and we aimed at the front door of the hospital.

The next few days were terrible for me. But at last the mail caught up and I got his first letter. I had already written two and was about to mail the third when I picked up his first words from Switzerland.

"I feel better already," he wrote. "And I love you more than ever! I'll be back for you by Christmas!" In the envelope he sent a little white card. On it he fastened a few little white blossoms--Edelweiss, a sign of eternal faithfulness. I laughed and cried to myself in my room that night. I held and caressed the little white card when I was alone. I put it in my dresser on top of my one pair of treasured real silk stockings, given to me by Frau Kamm. (They hadn't fit her, she said. I always suspected she was really just giving me a present).

Our letters were full of love, just as our conversations had been. But he complained often that his parents seemed set against us ever marrying. They still maintained the old objection that I wasn't a Catholic girl. But when he suggested I might convert, they had not softened at all.

I knew the truth clearly enough. I wasn't fit to marry their son. That's what they thought. I was too poor. I was only volksdeutsche, foreign-born, raised on a farm. I wasn't good enough. That was it.

I never said this in any of my letters to him. He never spoke a word of such ideas to me in his own missives. In this respect we already had begun to build a gulf between ourselves across which we dared not communicate. Still he implored me to see what a desperate situation he was in. His parents were saving his very life! If not for their support, he never would have gotten to Davos. He probably would have died in a German hospital, perhaps in my arms right in Melsungen. Could I see what a debt he owed to his family? I could see clearly. I owed them his survival just as he did. Could I understand his reluctance to enter into a great battle with them, his fear that it would seem ungrateful and inconsiderate? I could.

His letters were full of anguish. He hadn't realized how strongly they felt until they came for him. Their conversation lasted all the way to Switzerland. If he ever went on to finish medical school as he so passionately wanted to do, he would need their support. He wasn't certain what they would do if he married me anyway, but he felt torn between his love for me and his loyalty to his family, his desire not to hurt them.

The summer of 1938 had only just begun when I realized something was gone. Our relationship had died, or had been lost, or perhaps abandoned. His letters were less frequent. Mine were less frequent, too. There was nothing new to say. He had slipped away from me. His family had reabsorbed him. He perhaps had not even admitted it to himself openly yet, but it was clear enough to me.

I could have felt bitter and cheated, but I loved him so much, too much to feel angry in any way. I only felt lost and sad. Rudi was torn away from me by disease and family. I had held my dreams in my hands, but so briefly! Like the spring blossoms they seemed to be withering and crumbling.

I was walking at the center of Melsungen one warm summer morning when Frau Kamm emerged from a shop directly in my path.

"Good morning, Klara!" she greeted me cheerily. But she must have noticed something in my eyes, in my expression. ""Why, what's wrong, Klara? Is something wrong at home?" I could see her first guess was my mother's eyes again.

"No," I reassured her. I told her that my mother's recovery continued. I felt embarrassed to tell her about my personal problems, but after all she had done for me, it would have been wrong to keep things from her. It took me a moment to reply. "I fell in love."

Neither of us said anything for a second. A host of expressions flitted across her face, finally settling into a look of almost amused understanding, verging on pity. From most people, such a look would have made me angry, but I knew she cared about me. I only felt more foolish.

"Oh, Klara." She put her arm around me, and guided me into a slow walk with her along the street. "And it's over already?" I nodded my head slightly. "Oh, you poor girl." We walked until we reached the middle of the little foot bridge over the river, and stood looking down into the placid waters slipping by. Finally she spoke again.

"Listen, Klara, you have always talked about being a nurse. But what you're doing now isn't really nurses' training."

Since she had put me onto the work at the hospital, she knew perfectly well that it was only a helper's job, not a real training program. I shook my head to acknowledge her statement.

"Well, why don't you apply for the real nurses' training program at the hospital? You certainly have proved yourself to them with your work there so far. They know you now, and I suppose they like you well enough."

This audacious idea never had occurred to me. Leave it to a woman like Frau Kamm to be so bold, so direct, so logical. Though it was a long shot I had to admit that it made sense. We continued walking and talking, but already my life's direction had taken another sudden change, and again it had been caused by just a few words from this woman.

I talked about the idea with my mother, and with Marta, and even with Sister Konstanza. I also wrote a letter to Rudi, though I hadn't heard from him for some time by that point. I reasoned to him that I might as well study nursing while waiting for him to get well. That was what I told him. To myself, even as I wrote the letter, I was more candid. I knew it was over. The romance which had blossomed so suddenly with the spring flowers also had blazed out almost as quickly as they had fallen from the trees and bushes. All that was left of my love of a lifetime was a little white card with some fragile, dried petals fastened to it, carefully tucked away in a drawer in my bedroom. I felt sure I could never find another to take the place of Rudi in my heart. No love could be so clear, so strong, so enveloping. Like the sisters I had come to know in Melsungen, perhaps I would dedicate my life to selfless service to others. It was wonderful if a little fanciful to see myself in that light.

So I filled out the formal application at the hospital, and then went on with my ordinary days. The radio room, pushing wheelchairs on the lawn, working in the kitchen, all my tasks remained the same. Memories of Rudi in the midst of them faded slowly in my heart and gradually began to cause me less pain. I even

Klara as queen of the ball, 1938

joined a dancing class and practiced different syles of dance. It was a lot of fun; I loved to dance! At the end of the class they had a "grand ball" for all the participants—without a romance in my life, I relied on my brother Otto to be my partner for that event. I must have learned my lessons well, for the crowned me the queen of the ball for the way we danced the tango. They even gave me a little crown, but made me take it off for the photograph that celebrated the event.

The summer of 1938 passed into fall. It seemed almost impossible that only a year had passed since leaving the Kamm household. I felt I had lived through at least a decade! I was a much different person from that first morning when I walked up the hill to the hospital. For some reason I grew more and more certain that I would be accepted into the nurses' training program. Indeed, when the letter finally arrived I almost felt there was no need to open it. I knew I would be accepted, and I was.

By that winter, I had dived deep into the lessons and practical training. It was still the same hospital, but I found myself in rooms and situations I had never seen before in my earlier duties. We lived in rooms right in the hospital, since most of the trainees were from other cities. I was one of the few local girls admitted to training that year. Many of us quickly struck up new friendships, sitting in our rooms and looking out at snowy landscapes as the days grew shorter.

Klara

Our work moved ahead steadily. I felt more experienced with each passing day. We learned more and more of the job of nursing, though we worked only in the wards. In addition to our wards there were quite a few private rooms for special patients, but none of us in the training program worked there. Those patients were the responsibility of the regular nurses.

The head nurse who supervised us was a big, powerful woman. She looked like a man, to tell the truth. She ruled us with an iron hand. First thing in the morning she made the rounds, hunting out each of us as we did our many jobs. She always made us stand up straight and look at her, as she inspected us with hard eyes and lips drawn tight in a flat line. Our hair always had to be parted in the middle, pulled back tightly and tucked under our nurses' hats. Our white and navy blue uniforms always had to be crisp and clean. Our black stockings had to be straight and our black shoes had to be shined. From her we got our tasks and worked until we finished them.

Once a week we each got half a day of free time. As a local girl, this put me in the excellent position of being able to show some of my new friends a side of Melsungen they never would have discovered on their own. When springtime arrived for 1939 and we could get about easily again, we visited some of the little shops and restaurants in the town. We sometimes went to the movies. A lot of the films we saw were made by UFA, the propaganda-producing company. The whole idea of the cinema was quite new in those days. German film makers were experimenting with this new way to reach out to a vast new audience. The Nazis were experimenting with ways to use the film makers. One film we watched was "The Great Love" starring Zara Leander. I thought Zara sounded like Klara. I tried to picture myself in her place. I still remember vividly how in that film she gave up one of her own eyes for her son. I remember her sacrifice.

They gave me a leave from my studies for a few days to go down the hill and stay at home with Mama. Hilda had turned fourteen while I had been preoccupied up in the hospital, and even had finished school and confirmation. I suddenly realized how little I had seen of them in recent months. She seemed much taller. I could begin to see outlines of an adult in her. That was a revelation after seeing her only as a little girl before. Even Aline had grown bigger. She was ten by that time. They sat with me at the old familiar table in our kitchen, and hung on my every word about life among the other nurses in training. We walked together through the town when we had errands to do.

Still, I kept thinking about my classes and my training, no matter how nice it was to stay at home again for a little while. I worried I was missing too much. So in a way it was a relief to see the leave draw to a close. It was a little interlude I will always treasure, but at the time I got a little impatient by the end of it. By this point, of course, letters from Rudi had stopped coming altogether. Still it was hard. I could still almost see his gentle grey eyes. I tried to remember what it had felt like to have his arms around me. Then if I did manage to remember, I tried to forget. The training program became my refuge from such memories, as well as a beacon pulling me toward my future. But bigger tides were running in those days, and no one's future turned out to be quite what they were expecting.

Chapter Four
THE WAR BEGINS

When we gathered in our rooms to talk, the nurses' training lessons we were trying to master often led to anxious discussions. But of course we also gossiped about the doctors and nurses in charge of our program. It wasn't unusual for conversations to turn to handsome young men who might appear from time to time as patients in the wards, but with my memories of Rudi I was completely immune to those conversations. This was not something that would come up in my life again. I felt quite strongly about that.

But once in a while, we also found ourselves talking about the wider world of politics and national affairs. One of the girls even had read Hitler's book, *Mein Kampf*, though she didn't like the Nazis. She was from a good family and felt that such riff-raff were beneath her station in life. She told me about how Jews were losing their homes, their jobs and their businesses. She couldn't understand why they all wanted to go to America, where she thought they all were going.

"Look at all these stories about Czechoslovakia in the newspaper," she said one day, pointing at the front page. Three million Germans, according to the newspaper stories, were suffering terrible discrimination and abuse in Czechoslovakia. Soon enough, Hitler announced that two provinces of Czechoslovakia were being "rescued" by Germany. Almost before we knew it, Czechoslovakia was gone. The Third Reich lay sprawled all across central Europe. The anti-Polish hysteria in the movies we watched on our half-days in town grew louder and more extreme. Each day the newspapers blared out shrill banner headlines.

"It's hard to believe," one of the girls remarked one day, as we walked back up to the hospital from an afternoon in town. We could see and hear the tension in people's faces and conversations. "Just see how excited everybody is--some of them are almost frantic!"

And yet somehow it still shocked and surprised nearly all of us when German armored spearheads, supported by massive air strikes, attacked across the border into Poland.

Britain and France declared war on Germany.

It didn't seem possible, but suddenly it had begun in earnest. At first nothing really changed around us, but we definitely were at war.

The grim proof was not long in arriving. From the first invasion to the final collapse, the whole battle for Poland fit into September 1939 with time to spare. But this startling new lightning war was not without costs. We didn't see the blitzkrieg. We saw its aftermath, as did hospitals across Germany.

Not long after the war erupted into reality, the first truck arrived filled with wounded men. At first we had enough beds, but their wounds were horrible. This was not the same as the neat surgical stitches and incisions left by our doctors. I finally had gotten used to seeing such marks on the patients. But wounds were something quite different, something I never got used to.

The very first wounded man I helped had had his left arm blown off and amputated to the elbow in a field hospital. Supervised by one of the staff doctors, one of our interns checked, cleaned and reclosed the stump of the man's arm. The neat stitches he left contrasted strangely with the sight of only half an arm dangling from the young man's shoulder. It was my first close look at war. I didn't like it.

Many more wounded men arrived. As quickly as we could, we patched up the least serious cases and released them. Some others stayed on a longer time, or sometimes were transferred to another hospital in a different city. Sometimes I went along with several nurses to accompany some of the more serious cases when they were transferred, handing them over to other nurses in the train stations of other cities. A few died, but not many. If they made it all the way back to our hospital, they were likely to survive their immediate ordeals.

The first time a local boy died there, a boy who I had seen in the schoolyard and who I tended as he lay in the hospital, a pain of shock and hurt cut through me. The horror of his death struck me harder because I had known him. Each new death hurt, though, and I never reconciled myself to such tragic losses.

By the time the first snow fell in 1939, new casualties dwindled away to an infrequent trickle and finally dried up altogether. If the war continued to reap its grim harvest, at least we were no longer seeing it directly. After a sudden outburst of violence in the fall, the war seemed to curl itself up somewhere for the winter and go into hibernation.

Klara

Also nearly over was our training to become nurses! In the spring of 1940, just before my birthday in early April, we officially finished the program and received our nursing certificates. War or no war, one of my most cherished dreams had come true. I really was a nurse at last! On April 8th I rode the train with several other "new nurses" to a very fancy restaurant in nearby Kassel. We had a special banquet to celebrate. Someone even arranged to have a wonderful torte brought out for my birthday dessert. I had reached the magic number, twenty years old.

The next day Germany invaded Norway from the skies and the sea. War returned with the spring. In May the western blitzkrieg was unleashed against Belgium, the Netherlands and France. Again it took only a few weeks. By early June the British had fled from Dunkirk, Paris fell to our armies, and by late June France was knocked out. It was Poland all over again. There seemed to be no stopping us. German armies simply went wherever they wanted to go. Germany and Italy together had overwhelmed all of western Europe in less than a year. Spain was already friendly. Only Britain remained to carry on the war.

Nurses were needed desperately. Even after my training ended officially, they kept me working in the hospital. I got a letter from Otto while I was there. He had gone to Norway with the occupation forces as a motorcycle messenger in the infantry. As the seasons changed and winter smothered the landscape again, life at the hospital followed its familiar routine. We didn't get many casualties for a long time. There always seemed to be a few, though, and some stayed for weeks.

Then early in 1941 the horrible side effects reappeared at our hospital when German armies swept down over the Balkans. This time the German troops had not only Austrians fighting alongside them, but Italians as well, and later even Hungarians and eventually Romanians. We even saw one or two casualties from those other countries. A Hungarian soldier named Laszlo was brought in, very badly wounded, and for some reason the head nurse thought that because I spoke Russian I might be able to understand him. I was brought into his room, but of course neither of us could understand a word the other said and they sent me away again.

But then came the biggest shock of all. One June morning we woke up to the news, blaring from every radio, that a huge invasion had erupted across the Russian borders from Finland to Romania, shattering the quiet of the eastern front. For the rest of 1941 the reports from Russia sounded just like the 1939 campaign in Poland or the 1940 campaign in France. German armored spearheads drove the Russians before them like straws in the wind. But Russia was inconceivably bigger than Poland or France. Month after month the fantastic advance surged forward, and still only a fraction of Russia's immense territory had been crossed. By the end of the year the armies at the front were about a thousand kilometers from Berlin.

As more and more wounded men filtered back out of Russia, the current growing stronger with each passing month, our mood changed. Talking in the corridors dwindled. Laughter seemed to vanish altogether. No one seemed able to foresee any happy times ahead. In fact, the climate of fear grew not just from the evident intensity of the fighting but from things that happened there in the hospital, too. The most frightening of these was the way people would simply disappear once in a while. A nurse, or sometimes even a doctor, would be there one day, and then the next day they were gone. No one asked any questions, no one talked about it. I still don't know what was happening there.

In the midst of all these world-shaking events, added troubles suddenly appeared down the hill in my own home. Mama was having difficulties with her eyes again. I tried to get down to see here as often as I could. All through the winter carrying 1941 into 1942 I often

Klara, Hilda, Aline 1939

Klara

slept in my own old bed at home, under my own thick feather quilt. At Christmastime we got another short, battered letter from Otto, who had gone with his unit from North Africa and now was deep inside Russia. He didn't say much. He wrote about building a fire under his motorcycle so the motor would start. Mama nodded her head when I read that part out loud--she remembered the Russian winters perfectly well.

The walk to the hospital took me about half an hour most of the time. I was never late for work that winter. I worked in that hospital for most of the first half of 1942, sometimes in daylight and sometimes on a night shift. When I worked at night, I could sleep for a bit in the morning and then get up and spend the afternoon with Mama around the house. I watched my mother carefully, seeing her in new ways all the time, marveling at all she had managed to do to hold our family together through all our turbulent times.

One day at about lunchtime we were sitting down at the table. A bicycle bell rang in the street. I watched Mama walk out to take the little envelope.

"It's for you, Klara! It's from the work bureau down at the train station."

I stood up and took the message.

"What is it?"

It was a summons. It had come through the local work bureau, all right, but it was from Kassel. I was ordered to report to the central post office building. The following day I took the train to Kassel. There I walked through the town to a great red brick post office building. A light mist was falling. I shivered in my summer dress.

Inside I asked directions, showing my letter, and was directed to a short side hallway. An open door was visible at its end. Inside the door I glimpsed the front of a big desk. Behind the desk sat an SS-man in his uniform.

My heart gave a little flutter in my chest. Outside the door stood another SS-man, wearing a shiny helmet and holding in one hand the leash of a large German shepherd. This dog never moved a muscle nor made a sound. It only turned its head slowly, following me with its eyes. I approached the guard in the hallway to explain why I was there. He looked at the note I had received and told me to go on in.

The fellow behind the desk barely looked up as I entered.

"Name?" he inquired, gesturing toward a chair. I told him, and sat down. By now I knew his type. He and the fellow who had interviewed me about a job in the suture factory years before were cast from the same insecure mold.

"You live in Melsungen?"

"Yes, that's right."

He made some notes on a sheet of paper in the open folder on his desk. Finally he looked up at me. It seemed strange, almost out of character, but he seemed to be trying to look friendly. He wasn't exactly succeeding.

"Oh, yes," he smiled a little apologetically, after we had done with the formalities of introductions. "You're the one who's a nurse, aren't you?"

"Yes, sir."

"Born in Russia, correct?"

I nodded to confirm his information. He called to the man in the hall to send in two other names. A moment later we were joined by two more SS officers. Taking me completely by surprise, they began with questions about my childhood in Russia. They wanted to know all about my relatives. They knew my brother was in the army. But did I have other relatives left in Russia? I told them the truth, that as far as I knew all of us who had not been shipped off in boxcars to Siberia already had come out. This seemed to be exactly what they wanted to hear. One of them nodded to the other, who leaned over and said something to the man behind the desk. The two of them left as mysteriously as they had arrived.

"Well, I'm afraid you won't be doing any nursing for a while now. You start next week in a training program for radio operators," my interviewer declared. "Your language skills are important."

"Radio operators?" I echoed. My confusion must have been plain.

"You know the big Kassel-Rotewesten air base?"

I nodded that I did.

"There is a communications center in the basement of this very Post Office building, where radio operators keep the base in contact with the rest of the Luftwaffe," he explained. "That is where you will be trained. You don't have to be back here until next Tuesday for the first meeting. Why don't you go home again and just relax for a few days?"

I nodded hesitantly. He dismissed me and I left.

He was quite pleasant and polite about it all, but clearly the fatherland wasn't interested in my nursing plans. They needed radio operators. I would be a radio operator.

When I got home again I explained it all to my family. Just like on any other day, we worked our little garden, and hung out the washing, and kept the house clean. But over the next few days I couldn't stop thinking about my new assignment.

The following week arrived quickly enough. I rode the train back to Kassel again, trying to feel ready for my first lesson at being a soldier. Crossing the Standeplatz to the Post Office, I quickly found myself in the midst of a throng of other young women. None of us had uniforms yet. We gathered in a knot by one wall, in the large basement room where we had assembled.

Finally a young Luftwaffe officer came in behind us. After a rather formal greeting, he made his way to a long raised platform along the far wall, which ran the length of the room. We girls glanced at each other approvingly. A nice handsome instructor was a fine start! His blue-grey uniform made him look very dashing. We came forward and fanned out to sit at the long tables filling the center of the room.

"All right, ladies, I will be your first instructor," he began. "Once you have learned to use your radio equipment you will become part of a radio net reaching all over the continent, carrying information about all the activities of our Luftwaffe and of any enemy planes which might try to attack us. With your help, we will be able to launch our planes against any invaders."

There was a good deal more of this. Eventually we understood that a whole string of observers along the coast kept radio contact with major air bases inside Germany. This was all before radar, so it was the best one could do for air defense.

Not much time was spent on such general information. The first practical item we had to face was memorizing codes and symbols of air navigation, a whole language of its own. Up on the front platform our instructor wrote things on a huge glass screen. We spoke into microphones, repeating the names and messages again and again.

Our equipment also required some attention. We had to learn how to adjust the headsets we wore, and where to go in the building for spare equipment if a headset or microphone should malfunction. A more alarming piece of our training involved defense drills. One day, a new instructor came in with a great armload of gas masks and passed them out to us.

"Now," he called when he was finished, "if I can have your attention we will learn how to use these masks. If there should ever be an air raid, you may need them." They smelled new and rather unpleasant, but we had to practice putting them on and breathing through them. There was plenty of giggling at how strange we looked sitting there like giant insects, breathing solemnly. Then, masks still on, we were led in a bizarre-looking column through an evacuation drill of the building. Heads turned when we filed out into the street! Back inside our lecture continued.

"In most cases we would not have enough warning for you to go anywhere if you left the building," he said. "Really the safest place in town is probably right here in this basement. If there ever was a raid on Kassel, you would do well to just stay right here."

In the end we knew so much terminology, so many symbols, we developed a strange conversational style among ourselves. All of the classes were held at night. Spending days in Melsungen with my family, sleeping much of the morning, I rode the train to Kassel after dinner in the evenings. There I sat through the night, a set of headphones on my head, facing a microphone in front of me.

My job was quite simple once all of the codes and symbols were understood. I shared one of the long tables with forty-five or fifty other girls, each talking to an opposite number in some distant city. Up on the large clear screen on the front platform, several men moved back and forth making little marks for us to read. The wires from their own headsets snaked about on the platform as they worked.

I had to read long strings of numbers and letters into my microphone. On the other end of the line, a girl in a similar room in Koblenz repeated each string back to me to be sure she got it right.

Klara

And so it would go. When we weren't preaching strings of numbers and letters to each other, the girl in Koblenz and I also managed to talk a little in an ordinary way. She told me about radio conversations she sometimes heard between her center and the crews manning the anti-aircraft batteries around Koblenz.

I settled quickly into the routine of this new life. Night would fall. The little farming villages and towns around Kassel would light up (behind heavy shutters) for a little while. Then everyone would go to bed and fall asleep. Except a few of us, that is, who filed into our bright underground room. We sat down at our long tables, put on our headsets and began to recite.

I spent a lot of time daydreaming after a while. It got to the point that reciting messages became almost automatic. I reflected on the contrast between the darkened, sleeping countryside outside and my own little world of lights and distant voices coming over the wires.

I saw similar contrasts when I came off duty in the mornings. As I walked through the streets to catch a train home each morning, Kassel awakened around me. Already tired from the long night, the endless task of transmitting, the bright lights, I felt out of step with the morning faces of people hurrying this way or that. They magnified my feelings of weariness, of being used up. It was as though I had been emptied of substance already while everyone else was packed full of vital energies and ready to face the day. People went about their ordinary business, some to work and others to market, just as the morning occupants of Kassel's streets always had. But here and there one might also come upon groups of soldiers marching down a street, rifles slung at their shoulders. These little uniformed bands in one way looked perfectly natural, at least after a while. But they also struck me sometimes as very strange, something I only imagined was intruding on the little city.

If not entirely believable as an impression of Kassel, this feeling of still being in the past somewhere, not really in the war at all, was certainly true for Melsungen. First of all I enjoyed a morning train ride to get there, rattling past factories and houses of Kassel which quickly gave way to pleasant rolling countryside. Little hills and patches of forest alternated with good farmland. Morning light seemed to wash the countryside clean. Just when the quiet landscape had done its soothing work, and I was feeling quite removed from the war in the Kassel basement, the train pulled into the station at Melsungen.

Off to the right the Fulda River coiled through the town, spanned at the bottom of the hill by two old bridges. One was for traffic and the other so old and narrow it was only good for pedestrians and bicycles. Then the road wound back uphill, passing under the railroad through a concrete tunnel, and led up a diagonal along the slope. There our house sat in a row with the others, a Nazi suburb where only a field had been just a few years before. The other side of that street was still pasture, ending in trees further up toward the crest of the ridge. The scenery here hadn't changed with the coming of the war. The town sat where it always had.

From my months in the hospital, though, I could remember so many young men whose shattered bodies gave evidence to the reality of the war. Even inside my home I could see the differences in this familiar tapestry. Otto was gone, far afield with the war machine. Thus I vibrated between the realities of a world much changed by the marshalling of the German people into armies, and surface images of an unchanged, peaceful world surrounding us like painted background scenery.

In this fashion, sleeping in the day and reciting symbols through the night, riding trains back and forth, I scarcely felt the weeks go dancing past. But I will never forget the first night I watched the symbols gradually point straight at Kassel itself. I recited into my microphone, my voice calm, my hands steady. I saw the ranges decreasing, the swarm of fighters from Rotewesten appear on the screen and intercept. With my headset on, of course I never heard any droning of planes overhead, and anyway we were inside the basement of the big post office building. No sounds could reach us there.

Then suddenly my voice broke off in mid-sentence. There was an unmistakable, momentary vibration in the floor, the table, the big screen, everything. Everyone was glancing at one another. More tremors followed. We continued our recitations. After a barely perceptible pause the men on the platform continued to write.

The next morning I got on the train for my usual ride home to Melsungen. Suddenly, out the windows of the train I caught sight of several houses blackened and gutted by fire, people swarming over the ruins. The bombers had been after the rail lines. They missed.

The next night, I remember very well, was much quieter than usual in the communications room. Nobody talked much except to transmit messages. Even then voices were quieter. We seemed to think that if only we could keep our voices down we would be less likely to be chosen as a target again. Totally unreasonable, of course, but people will behave in some odd ways when they suspect enemy airplanes may soon fly over their heads and try to blow them all to bits with bombs.

By the end of 1942 the Russian front was twice as far away as the previous year, two thousand kilometers or more from Berlin. Was there no end to Russia? Was it simply too big to swallow? One of the guards in the basement hallway commented that Germany was like a shark. First it had eaten all the little fish--Poland, Austria, Czechoslovakia, and so on. Now it was trying to swallow a whale.

The tide was turning against us in Russia that winter as we entered 1943, though at first it didn't seem that way. Suddenly the fighting raged up more fiercely than ever, instead of tapering off as it had in earlier winters. We heard vague, unsatisfactory reports about "heroic resistance" against what we guessed must be a massive Russian winter attack around Stalingrad. The fighting raged. The German army was forbidden to withdraw, unlike the Russians who had traded immense chunks of the Ukraine for time and rest during the powerful German advances. I prayed for Otto over and over again. Like bare branches left to face the winter wind alone when all the leaves have fallen, we began to feel very alone and exposed in that little town, though the buildings and the river and all the rest of the scenery was just as it always had been.

I worked in Kassel until October of 1943, until one autumn day my morning walk from the basement room to the train station marked the beginning of the end of my tenure there. I boarded the train in Kassel to return home. The fields gliding past the window looked golden as golden should truly be. Even the cows seemed to catch the mood, lying in the warm scented grass and sleeping.

When I got home I helped mother hang out some washing to dry in the sun. We had a good mid-morning breakfast together. I felt an enormous, unexplainable drowsiness flooding over me that morning.

I'm sure that even without encouragement from every side, my uncanny longing to sleep would have done its work unaided. I went to bed after lunch and slept as though I were drugged. The afternoon passed, and stretched out into a crisp autumn evening. Still I did not waken.

Finally Mama came upstairs to get me up. She had been calling me to no avail. I could hardly open my eyes. I was groggy and incoherent. At last she urged me out of bed and down the stair, and sat a cup of "coffee" made from ground-up grain in front of me.

"Klara!" she repeated, exasperated. "You'll be late for work!"

This last thought finally penetrated my brain, but it still took a moment before I could force myself into any reaction.

"You have to get dressed or you'll miss the train!" she exclaimed.

I awoke fully to a panic that I might indeed miss the train. Racing upstairs, I pulled on my uniform in a most unsatisfactory manner and ran out the door without any supper.

But I missed the train. Even as I came running down the hill I heard the whistle screech. The engine magnified its grumbling. The train pulled away from the station. I was stuck. I could not get to work. We had no telephone either. I could not even call Kassel. I wondered what was going to happen to me, as I plodded back up to the house, frustrated and more than a little frightened about my truancy.

It grew dark and I sat with my mother in the kitchen, thinking about the brightly-lit room and my empty chair. Of course someone else would fill it, but it would cause a disturbance.

At last my mother broke the silence.

"Now you see how it is for me to sit here every night," she said, in a quiet, wistful voice. At that moment I think I appreciated her loneliness as I never had before. "I sit here worrying about all of you, each one off in a different crazy place." I moved closer and hugged her.

And as if this remark were some sort of prearranged signal, suddenly we could barely discern the shaking of explosions outside in the night air.

Klara

We ran out to the front walk.

The sky to the northwest toward Kassel was lit with searchlight beams in the distance. The flash of explosions and the red glow of fire flickered over the horizon. The bombs were coming down on Kassel again! There were also sparks of flak in the sky, and from time to time the noise of the bombing drifted faintly down the skies on a night breeze to our straining ears. Below us, at the base of the hill, the town was completely dark.

Except for our own front door, gaping open, gushing out a flood of light! How stupid! We rushed back inside and closed the door.

It wasn't until late the next day that I learned how bad the attack had been. They had been after more than the railroads this time. The October 1943 RAF attack on Kassel is known today as one of the heaviest bombing raids conducted up to that point in the war. Several bombs scored direct hits on the post office. It was smashed flat. Not a brick was left standing. Everyone in the basement had been killed.

Kassel after October 1943 RAF night bombing raid

It was some days before the Luftwaffe understood that I wasn't in the basement that night, that I wasn't dead. Of course I had to report in within a day or I would have been counted as a deserter, and the penalty for that was death, but even after reporting it took some time for them to realize where I was.

I spent many hours in following days thinking about my uncanny drowsiness. Again it seemed something more than mere chance had been taking a hand in my life, guiding my footsteps, keeping me safe. A guardian angel? More than once I walked down into town. I sat by myself inside the old grey stone Lutheran church, thinking.

Chapter Five
BIELANY

After the terrifying destruction in Kassel, I had one more interview about my career as a radio operator. I hadn't finished the training program. At first I feared they might send me off somewhere to begin that all over again as well, just the way my year of arbeitsdienst had to be repeated. But they told me I had completed enough of the program. I was finished, trained. They were not quite ready to assign me someplace, though.

I remembered how girls already in training when I started had gone off to various new posts when then they finished the program. Most went to other cities in Germany. But two of them had gone to France--one big heavy girl, and one tiny doll-like girl. They both spoke French fluently. I seem to remember another girl who spoke Dutch, who had gone to Holland when her training was complete. But I spoke Russian! Surely they weren't going to send me back into Russia!?

In the meantime I was sent to work as a nurse again, this time in the same great white hospital in Kassel where my mother's eye surgery had taken place. I couldn't really live at home any more then. We had to go around to the back of the hospital, where rooms for staff were available in a side wing. I lived there in Kassel, in the hospital itself, and before I knew it I found myself immersed once again in the work I knew and loved. After I had been there for a couple of weeks, I began to dare to think that perhaps they would forget all about my radio operator career, and just let me go back to being a nurse again. After all, I hadn't really finished the program. Trained nurses were important, too, weren't they?

Blasting one building flat couldn't affect my place in the larger scheme of things for long, though. I managed to travel home and spend a day or so with my family once in a while. It was during one such visit, just when I had finally begun to get my hopes up about being left alone in nursing, that a young bicycle messenger dressed in a uniform far too big for him brought a packet of papers to our gate one evening. They turned out to be my new orders.

The girls who had been scattered all over the continent came back to me then, and I remembered what the SS man had said about my Russian language being valuable. Still, I was startled by what I read--Warsaw!

I was going to Warsaw. After all these years, I was being ordered back to the very doorstep of Russia. Well, it made sense after all. Who spoke Russian better than someone raised in Russia for thirteen years?

The orders were very terse. Nothing about what my new assignment would be. I could guess I would be wearing radio headphones, and that there would be airplanes in the picture somewhere. Beyond this I knew nothing. With the orders came a passport for me, since I would be leaving the territory of Germany proper. A number was stamped in the back of it.

Mama walked down to the train with me. Neither of us knew if we would ever set eyes on each other again. We hugged goodbye bravely but a few tears did escape. I looked back as my train pulled away, leaving her standing with a little crowd of other people on the platform beside the tracks. Today I wonder how she ever stood it. She looked sad beyond belief.

Train travel was pretty unnerving by this time. The train was crowded full of people of every description, all thrown together by their urgent need to get somewhere. Several times along the way we were delayed by air raid damage to the tracks. In Berlin, while I wandered in the great bahnhof waiting for a new train, I heard sirens in the city outside. We didn't leave the train station, though. I guess the attack was centered in another part of the city.

All this bombing and other interference, unfortunately, made me nearly a day and a half late getting to Warsaw. The train car in which I rode was quite crowded but I felt terribly lonely. I didn't know where to go, or what to do. I was wearing my nurse's uniform, so everyone seemed to assume I knew my own business. This frightened me even more, because I had no idea what I was doing.

The train passed through the shadowy western suburbs in the darkness, stopping at an outlying station or two. There were no bright lights on the platform, no crowds in the stations. At last we drew up at a platform of the central station in the heart of the ancient city of Warsaw. People poured out of the cars, me in the middle of the crowd. A few other people, nearly all military officers, were already on the platform waiting to greet passengers.

All the voices I heard spoke in German in tense and quiet voices. I only heard a few words as we all crowded out of the train. What I did hear made my blood run cold, though. In those brief snatches of conversation I managed to overhear words about partisans, about the Polish underground, about how the city was very dangerous at night. Some of the soldiers on the platform, it turned out, were not there to meet people after all. They were there to order us off the platform, urgently moving us along. Everyone seemed nervous, afraid of some unseen threat. Even the main station showed almost no lights.

It was the middle of the night, not early afternoon as my schedule had instructed. In fact it was the wrong day altogether. No one paid any attention to me. Suddenly I noticed people were hurrying away in ones and twos at an alarming rate. In what seemed like no time at all I found myself on an almost deserted railway platform.

Alarmed, I rushed down into the passageway under the tracks. My shoes rang on the cold ceramic tiles of the tunnel floor. Hurrying into the station itself, I discovered to my dismay that it too stood hollow and nearly empty. Faces of a few officials looked out from behind some of the little windows along the walls but most were closed and dark. Almost no one was on the open floor itself. I shivered.

A German soldier was walking guard duty around the inside of the station. He stopped when he saw me looking around, and told me tersely to move on out of the station. No one was allowed in the station. There was a curfew. I tried to protest that I had no idea where I was supposed to go, that I was lost and alone, that I had arrived at the wrong time.

He didn't listen. He just escorted me out the great front doors. They slammed shut behind me. Terrified, I stood looking back inside for a moment but he looked back at me and made an angry shooing motion with his hand. He just wanted to be rid of me, to get me away from there.

But where could I go!? The night wind gusting down the broad boulevard whipped at my face and my uniform, forcing my breath back into my throat. Or perhaps it was my fear choking me. I turned around, numb with fright, and looked up and down the front walls of the station building desperately. The dark, empty street confronted me. On the far side of this wide boulevard, tall grey buildings loomed in rows, marching away east toward the Vistula and west toward the suburbs through which we had come. I stood and looked northward into the heart of Warsaw. Not a sound came to my ears from that direction.

Deciding that the hollow station offered me no help, at length I left the sheltering entrance and walked hesitantly down this darkened avenue a little way. What should I do? I had counted on some kind of military contact, someone to tell me what to do and where to go. Now I was completely abandoned in a hostile, dangerous city in the middle of the night.

For a moment, I had the uncanny impression that the whole city lay deserted with only me wandering about alone in the middle of it. I walked a little further along the sidewalk, but each step grew shorter and more timid. Finally my fear and the cold, windy darkness nearly paralyzed me altogether. I stepped into a recessed doorway, the door behind me covered from top to bottom with heavy boards nailed across it to seal it shut. I hugged my arms around myself and wished I were anywhere else in the world except alone on that boulevard.

The streets didn't stay empty, though. I heard indistinct noises from the direction in which I had been walking. I tried to shrink even further back into the deepest shadow of the doorway. The noise resolved itself into a group of men coming up the street, talking. The tread of their boots and an occasional rattle and clatter of weapons told me they were soldiers.

I heard a bit of German in the conversation.

It seemed like my only hope. But they mustn't mistake me for a partisan! I didn't want them to panic and shoot me. Forcing down the fear in my throat, I made myself step slowly out in front of them.

"Good evening," I managed to whisper, in a very small voice.

Klara

The soldiers jumped. They were nearly as nervous and scared as I was. Their training was excellent, though. They didn't shoot me to pieces. They only froze, some staring at me, some scanning nearby windows and doorways anxiously to make sure I was alone. Their rifles swung slightly in my direction without quite pointing at me. I held out my passport to the closest man and explained about my orders, the bombing, and the delay.

He listened, along with the nearest others. Alarm and tension in their eyes grew into disbelief. They were astonished to find a lone, unarmed German woman wandering around the streets of Warsaw in the middle of the night. They believed me, though, and so there was nothing to do but take me along with them. We walked for a very long time, until at last we got back to their command post.

That was more like it! Inside the low room a tiny light finally offered a small circle of relief from the fearful darkness. Perhaps a dozen soldiers in all were coming and going on night patrols. The corporal, whose name was Kurt, sat me down at a table, got me something hot to drink, and sat down to keep me company while the radio man tried to track down some information about what to do with me. They had figured out from my passport that I had something to do with the Luftwaffe, so they wanted to try and call them about me.

Kurt explained that things were pretty tense just then. From time to time there would be gun battles between the German occupation forces and the Polish underground. People were killed every day. He frowned as he told me I might not have survived through that night if partisans had found me first. The knot of tension and fear in my stomach tightened again. My frightful, lonely arrival actually was over but I couldn't relax. My arms, my hands, moved in tight, nervous motions.

Thankfully, it wasn't long before the radio man came back into the room.

"Well, we know where you're supposed to go," he said. "But we can't take you there. We're on duty. We have to wait until morning and someone will come down to pick you up. You might as well make yourself comfortable here."

I stayed awake for an hour or so after that, but eventually exhaustion from days on trains and the shock and fear of my solitary arrival caught up with me. I put my head down on my arms on the table and slept a little. It was very uncomfortable and my neck got very stiff.

They woke me in the morning. Sunlight was pouring into the room. The first sound I heard was a motor running out in the street. Four of the soldiers were ready to escort me to wherever it was I was supposed to be.

"The Luftwaffe couldn't send anybody this morning, so we're to drive you up to Bielany," the radio man remarked. The car turned out to be a little armored patrol car. Everyone carried guns except me. All the men seemed nervous. There had been a fight just the last night, while I had slept.

Bielany, they explained, was just about the last suburb to the north of Warsaw itself, on the west bank of the Vistula. The Luftwaffe had some kind of operation there, set up on the grounds of what had been a riding academy before the war broke out.

We drove a little way down the broad avenue in front of the train station. In daylight the great grey buildings no longer seemed threatening. They looked old and majestic, fit to stand at the heart of a historic European capital. Then we turned north into narrower streets. It took only minutes to reach the edge of the Jewish Ghetto. We were going to drive right through it.

Actually, it wasn't really there anymore. Buildings once crowded along those narrow lanes at the city's center, teeming with a Jewish population growing larger week by week. After Poland was divided by our armies and the Russians, Jews displaced from near and far moved in behind the walls of the ghetto.

Today we know that this mass of people then began to move out again, bit by bit, on trains to the death camps. The grisly task was accomplished by SS-men recruited from the dregs of Germany and of other conquered nations. Elderly leaders in the ghetto pursued their tragic policy of passive cooperation until only an explosive remnant remained. Then violence erupted. SS squads sent to round up the last Jews died in a hail of bullets. The SS responded overwhelmingly, brutally.

Klara

So though I couldn't understand why, as we drove into this area it seemed to me every building had been bombarded and wrecked, and then burned in the bargain. Here and there whole buildings still stood, but they were charred and grey. Smoke still drifted up into the sky above this devastation from fires smoldering deep within the larger ruins. Many houses were now only jagged bits of wall. Some were razed completely, leaving only a flat space of rubble.

Block after block of this sort of scene rushed past us. The little car roared down the deserted street. This terrible destruction couldn't be left over from the conquest of Poland, in the spring of 1941. Why would the ruins still be smoking so much later?

I was starting to ask about this, when a soldier in the front seat turned around. His eyes were distant, his expression harsh and scornful.

"You see here we're burning the pigs," he laughed.

"Pigs?" I asked.

"Those Jewish pigs," came the reply. His face registered an expression of disgust for these victims. He turned back to watch the street ahead, his rifle barrel leaned out over the door of the car.

The words struck me like a thunderclap. I must have turned quite pale. As I sat stiff and shocked, smoke continued to rise sedately at intervals from the charred ruins; from block after block of destruction and death. It was as if nothing had changed, as if the ugly soldier hadn't said anything. Successive blocks of rubble and burned-out buildings had no idea that suddenly they each horrified me more than the last.

But my world had been rattled to its foundations. These men in the car were on my side, citizens of my country! One of them may even have come from Kassel. Yet I found myself glancing at them as at the animals in the Kharkov zoo, as at some sort of outlandish creatures I had never glimpsed before.

At last we emerged from the north side of the ghetto. The giant charnel house vanished behind us. I hardly noticed. Eventually the grisly ride came to an end. Badly shaken, I climbed down from the car in front of a large gate set in a long wire fence. Both gate and fence had been thrown together from bare unplanned timbers and grey barbed wire. The little car roared away.

A very big man in a blue Luftwaffe uniform shouldered his way out of a small wooden guardhouse standing beside the gate. I pushed my papers though the barbed wire to him as we said hello. After glancing over them he swung the gate open. Expressionless, he pointed me across the grounds of the transfigured riding academy.

Straight ahead of me stood the main building of the academy. Two sidewalks curved across the wide lawn to meet at the front entrance. The building was built of red brick in the shape of a crescent, the ends curving toward me. Close by on the right, a second smaller brick building served as our dining room, as I later learned. Even further off to the right a third brick building stood at right angles to the first two. It was the officers' quarters.

Besides these permanent academy buildings, wooden structures had been added. One was just past the guardhouse on my left. The large painted red cross on a white circle on the eaves above the door marked it as the dispensary. The other, on the right between the dining hall and the front fence, was the women's barracks where the guard had directed me.

In that building I inherited a little cubicle. The building was carved up with unfinished boards into tiny rooms. A person could sleep and perhaps stretch out, but very little else. There were two beds in each room. Certain articles lying about on one side of mine indicated I already had a roommate. I lay down on the other bunk and even though it was still the middle of the day I fell into a deep sleep, exhausted and traumatized by my disrupted train journey, my sleepless night in the guard station, and the macabre ride through Warsaw.

Sometime later, I was awakened by a noise. It was probably a gasp of surprise. I sat up in the bed quickly. My roommate had returned from somewhere to find me like Goldilocks in the bed. I stood up politely and realized that this blonde girl was a little taller than me. At first I saw hints of a female version of Heinz Grauer from back in Melsungen--she definitely gave that first impression of a husky farm girl with her broad shoulders, her wide hips. How to put it discreetly? I later noticed that her problems with the bust sizes of our uniforms created a lot of interest from the men we worked with us in that compound. Yet her blonde hair always had a stylish cut. Her high cheekbones and beautiful eyes gave a classic beauty to her face.

"Hello!" she greeted me, as she sat down and pulled off her shoes. "My name is Erika. Who might you be?"

"Klara," I replied. We both sat down on our beds and made small talk for a while. I discovered that Erika was not actually from Germany, either. She grew up in in Riga, in Latvia. She was just as surprised to discover I grew up in the Ukraine. When she spoke, the farm-girl spell was broken. Erika spoke high German with a cultured, slightly old fashioned Latvian accent. Her laughter, clear and controlled, was the laughter of an intelligent woman. It didn't take me long to learn to like Erika very much. As we lived together in that room our friendship grew.

Almost as soon as I arrived, I was interviewed in a large room on the ground floor of the great curved main academy building. The officer who rose from his desk as I entered stood much taller than me. The orange shoulder boards on his uniform meant he was in the ground arm of the Luftwaffe; yellow was for the air arm.

In excellent Russian he introduced himself and invited me to have a chair near his desk. He asked where I was from, how I had come to Germany, and similar questions. We spoke only Russian. Of course he had all the answers to these questions in a little file somewhere in the office. The purpose of the interview was to observe my language skills at first hand.

Apparently he was satisfied with what he heard. He took my passport and stamped something into it, some kind of a seal. Then he told me I would be assigned to work there in the main building, up on the second floor. He called in an aide.

"Take this woman up to your room and present her to your commander. She will be assigned there," he ordered.

We saluted and left. He escorted me up a great wide marble staircase and down to the very end of the left hallway on the second floor. My guide opened a door to a room facing out the back of the building. We went in.

The huge room intimidated me, as did the eight or ten men inside, all high-ranking Luftwaffe officers preoccupied with their tasks. Three walls were plastered with great maps, some just tacked up over earlier ones. The fourth wall at the back provided three large windows, flanked by four or five desks where some of the officers sat working. A long, richly-paneled counter began at the wall next to the doorway where we entered, reached out into the room, and ended in an L-angle toward the far wall. More men were sitting at this counter. One seat was empty--mine.

"This is a listening room," advised my guide. "Here you will hear radio messages between Russian planes and their bases."

I looked around the room, wondering what I had in common with all these officers. It could only be the Russian language, and perhaps the jargon of air navigation. I was still wearing my nurse's uniform. One or two of them looked at me curiously. I didn't get my Luftwaffe uniform until the next day.

Glancing out the windows I saw the academy grounds sloping away behind the building. Down at the bottom of the gentle hillside, at a considerable distance from us, some sort of sprawl of small sheds, parked trucks, and great piles of crates and steel drums turned out to be a large munitions dump.

My job in this room proved to be exactly as described. I sat at the long, L-shaped counter. In the earphones on my head I listened to Russian voices, fighter pilots mostly. Certainly they were not flying over Warsaw. How the signal was brought to me there I cannot say. My training in Kassel and my childhood in Russia combined to make me perfect for the job, though.

As I listened to pilots talking, suddenly a voice for which we waited would break in.

"Gricha, Gricha. Answer, answer."

If there was no answer the sender immediately began swearing, a stream of profanity betraying the tension.

Then finally Gricha answered. A lot of words that made no sense at all passed back and forth. This coded message had to be copied down exactly, word for word. My transcriptions were rushed to another room, the decoding room. I never even found out where that was in the building. I had to wait for my replacement before I could leave the listening room.

This eavesdropping was only one part of the Bielany operation, but we never went into any room except the one in which we worked. We weren't even supposed to speak to anyone, except when doing our jobs. It was almost as though we were as afraid of each other as of the Russians. Once, though, I did hear one officer tell another that the Luftwaffe shot down forty planes using information we intercepted.

After my shift I usually dragged myself back to my room to relax, and then usually made my way over to the dining room. I always felt exhausted at Bielany. The work demanded such constant attention that it wore me out completely. Having Erika around made it bearable, though. The recreation room at the south end of our barracks gave us a perfect view of the door to the officers' quarters, and some of the twelve of us women in the camp went in and out of there quite a lot. Watching and keeping track of these assignations was about the only recreation we could find.

Erika came to Bielany because of her Russian language skills, too. Her family in Latvia had been rich, private and aristocratic, though, so she never mastered the language quite like a real Russian. We didn't talk about our jobs much, even off duty. The constant admonitions to keep our mouths shut proved quite effective.

The basement of the main building housed a modern Olympic-sized swimming pool, the first I ever saw. Before this I only knew swimming in the Kalmus and Fulda rivers. I didn't know how to swim. I had to be satisfied to sit on the steps at the shallow end, or hang on the side and kick my feet vaguely in the water. The other girls mostly could dive and swim at their pleasure.

That pool did give me an excuse to knit a daring brown and yellow bikini for myself, though! It was a funny thing about those swim suits. We always went down to the pool before we changed. In fact, for some reason we even had to swim in pitch darkness. Still, somehow the details of each of our swimming costumes soon became favorite topics in officers' conversations. How did they know? In the heat of that Polish summer the pool refreshed us all, even in the dark, and even for me, if only to take a dip in the water.

Erika and I also sat together in the cafeteria building. It was a congenial place, though conversation was restricted in the cafeteria because of the Poles. Several Polish civilians worked in the compound, despite the fact that it was one of the most tightly guarded secret installations in Warsaw. Most of them worked in the cafeteria cleaning floors, serving food, cooking and washing dishes. Some also did menial housekeeping chores in the officers' quarters. They officially weren't supposed to exist as far as we were concerned. We were discouraged from talking to them even in casual conversations. If you were reported for such talking, it could be trouble for you.

Yet I was drawn to one of the workers in the cafeteria. Small and delicate, she resembled a little porcelain doll. You could see in her face and her tiny, perfect hands that she wasn't used to hard work. Yet here she was in the Bielany kitchen, washing dishes and scrubbing floors on her hands and knees.

I've forgotten how it began. Despite our orders I found myself talking to her. I knew no Polish, but Polish is a distant cousin of the Russian language and she also knew some Russian herself. Slowly we got to know each other. It was the sort of acquaintance which springs up of its own accord between certain people, with even the stoniest soil in which to grow.

She had been the wife of a very high-ranking Polish officer, I found out. He was executed by our own army during the invasion three years before. Now she worked in ragged clothes, always keeping her eyes down on the floors. She was struggling to insure that her little son had food and shelter, to try to bring him and herself through the war alive. Once she took out a little locket. She showed me a picture of her husband and her little boy standing together. I looked at it and she put it away again quickly, next to her heart. Neither of us could say a word.

At other times, when we were relatively safe from eyes and ears that might report on us, she told me about their life together, what things had been like before the war began. She got a distant light in her eyes when she talked about those days. Her story came pouring out. I could tell how intense her loss must have been. She seemed to come to real life for a moment at such times. But she quickly retreated into a drab, eyes-down precaution after an instant of such escape into the past.

Since Erika and I spent so much of our free time there in the cafeteria it is not surprising that another event occurred in that setting, too. One day we were sitting together and talking about a trip back to Melsungen when a young officer came up to our table.

"Excuse me, ladies," he said. "May I join you?" He was extremely blond, almost pale. But there was no chance of mistaking this paleness for illness. Lean, taller than average, he looked very healthy and fit.

We nodded. He smiled his best charming smile and pulled up a chair to join us. Hans Marquardt was his name, we learned. In the course of the conversation we discussed all the latest rumors at the camp, but I couldn't help feeling he had some more specific goal in mind for the discussion. I was right, too. At length he finally asked me if I would like to go into the city with him and have dinner in a restaurant some time.

"How would we get there?" I asked.

"By streetcar," replied Hans. "Haven't you noticed? One runs past not far from the front gate." I had noticed, actually. Erika and I looked at each other knowingly. This was one of the basic approaches used when one of the men wanted to try to "get to know us better."

Erika nudged me with her elbow, just below the edge of the table where no one could see her. Smiling, I told him that would be very nice. He seemed pleased, and took his leave of us in a courtly manner.

"Klara, I'm impressed," Erika commented. "Several of the girls have been trying to get Hans to ask them what he just asked you. He's quite a fellow!"

"He is good looking," I agreed.

"And polite and interesting, too," she went on. "He comes from a rich family in Berlin."

"Oh, really?" I asked.

"Everyone seems to like him," she confirmed, and then added with a wink, "but what he sees in you I'll never know!" I made a face at her and we both laughed.

Hans and I left the compound together late one afternoon. We caught a streetcar outside the gate, and rode into the heart of Warsaw.

It was dangerous for German soldiers to roam about the city as we were doing. The Polish underground had picked Warsaw as a symbol of resistance to German occupation. We heard tales about Germans being pricked with poisoned needles on a crowded sidewalk, dying quickly from the poison. Such silent, clandestine attack was almost impossible to prevent or punish directly. Retaliation didn't seem to deter them, either. Big yellow sheets all over the city announced in bold black print that acts of terrorism against the German occupation would be answered with ten-for-one retaliatory public hangings. The ratio became twenty-to-one and still didn't deter the underground.

Warsaw streetcar 17 to Bielany

The streetcar had two cars, though, and the Poles could only jam into the second one. The first, reserved for Germans only, seemed nearly empty with only Hans and I, a couple of armed soldiers on guard, and two or three other passengers. I felt fairly safe as we began our trip.

The cafe turned out to be in an elegant hotel at the center of the city. The entire hotel had been turned into a German casino. Hans and I made our way past the heavily armed guards outside the entrance. In our dress uniforms, we found ourselves seated at a table out in the center of a large, ornate and crowded room. All around us soldiers of the Reich (chiefly officers) tried very hard to forget where they were for a moment and have a good time by drinking a lot. I looked up and admired the high ceiling of the place, which somehow had been contrived to look like a night sky with little points of light for the stars. I marveled at it.

Hans proved to be even more pleasant than Erika had suggested. We sipped our drinks and talked. He told me stories about the people in charge of the camp. I also learned how he had tried to get into the air arm of the Luftwaffe but wound up at Bielany instead. He had trouble with his eyes. That ruled out being a pilot. Beyond a few stories, though, he got me to do most of the talking. I liked him for that most of all, once I realized what was going on. He didn't spend the evening talking about himself. He really seemed interested in what I had to say. I came to like Hans more and more as our evening went on. The time flew by. We laughed and talked and ate our dinners.

Only much later did we notice we were among the last few couples in the whole wide ballroom. We had talked the whole evening away without noticing!

"I've lost track of time!" he laughed. "You see how you entrance me?"

Once he realized the hour, he suggested at once we should get back to camp. I had to visit the ladies' room before we left.

Our waiter directed me out into the foyer and up a stairway to the right. I followed the steps up to the restrooms and other anonymous doors on the floor above the ballroom. Just as I reached to open the door of the ladies' room, another door across the hall flew open. A Polish waiter stepped out directly in front of me. We were quite alone in the hallway.

His eyes locked onto mine. He just stood there, right in front of me. His black eyes burned like coals. He didn't move or speak—just that cold stare. I could read hatred in that stare. One step and he could reach me, seize me.

Perhaps he would have killed me if the encounter had lasted a moment longer. But suddenly another door opened, further along the hallway. The waiter jerked into motion and clattered down the stairs past me. I rushed straight back down behind him, afraid to go on into the bathroom.

Hans took me back to Bielany as quickly as possible after that. Before our evening on the town, I confess I had begun to feel suffocated inside the wire of the compound. No more! Any trace of such ideas was transformed into a sense of refuge and safety after that night. I went on no more adventurous dates into Warsaw.

The violence of a war swirling all around us could not be shut out of the Bielany compound, however. It always seemed to be able to find some new and terrifying form, each more disturbing than the last. Take the case of Doctor Mayer, a German officer in charge of the hospital on the grounds, tall, handsome, in his early forties. We all adored his Bavarian accent and his sense of humor. I liked him very much. He seemed to know everyone by name, and to be able to talk with each one of us about our own latest concerns. He took a particular liking to me after he found out I had been a nurse before my Luftwaffe days.

"We could have used you in the infirmary, too," he said wistfully. We could only guess at how overworked he was.

Later, one day I was walking back to the barracks after lunch in the cafeteria. I was going to meet Erika in our room when she came off duty. She told me at breakfast about some good news she had gotten from her family, but there had been no time to discuss it then.

Suddenly I looked up and found myself face-to-face with Doctor Mayer on the path. He was headed into the cafeteria as I came out. He looked ghastly. I froze in surprised alarm. His eyes looked hollow, haunted. His face, usually ruddy and cheerful, was as pale as ashes. I noticed, after absorbing this shocking sight, that all the insignia had been ripped off his uniform. The uniform coat was hanging open loosely. He stopped before me on the sidewalk. He seemed a ghost, an apparition standing cold and grey in the middle of the day.

"Doctor Mayer!" I cried.

In a voice as hollow and despairing as his eyes, he replied, "Goodbye, Klara. I will never see you again." Without a smile or a change of expression, he stepped past me and continued into the cafeteria building.

My heart nearly stopped. I didn't dare to run after him and ask him what had happened. All I could do was run toward the barracks, my heart still pounding. Before I had taken two steps, though, I spied Erika coming from the academy building. I rushed to intercept her before she reached the barracks.

"Erika!" I blurted out. "Something terrible has happened to Doctor Mayer! He's just gone into the cafeteria. His uniform is all torn, and he said he would never see me again! What can it be!?"

Klara

"You get back to the barracks," she decided at once. "I must go and talk to him." Erika was a very good friend of Doctor Mayer. This news of mine cast a shadow across her face.

She did go and speak to him, but I didn't learn the rest of the story for almost a day afterwards. She didn't even come back to the room that night to sleep. I grew nearly frantic with worry, waiting there alone. When she finally returned she volunteered nothing.

I didn't ask at first. I could see, though, that she was dying inside from the poisonous news she had learned. She had to share the pain and grief with someone. I finally asked her what had happened.

"I went to see him in the dining room," Erika replied slowly and quietly, as we sat down on our beds. "He was sitting all by himself at a table. No one else would sit with him. No one would even sit near him at another table. He was like a leper, Klara." She had to stop for a moment and collect herself. "The whole place was dead quiet. I tried to talk to him but he was in shock. Just numb. You saw how pale he was."

I nodded.

"Well, I only just got started talking to him, and they came in and got him. They just took him away yesterday afternoon."

"What?!" I cried.

"He gave a little medication to some of the Poles."

We looked at each other silently. What could anyone have said at that moment? After such an act? A lovely man. Dr. Mayer never had been too tired to get up in the middle of the night if someone were sick. He gave scarce medicine to Poles, as a doctor faced with their need. So they shot him. That was that. Later the usual spy rumors started about him, of course. That was the standard epilogue to any such story.

I don't understand it when I look back now. Such incidents should have frightened me to the point of paralysis. Certainly that was the intended purpose of such barbarism. And yet, some of the things I did were at least the equal of Doctor Mayer's fatal kindness. Perhaps my contact with the Poles in the compound allowed me to feel their humanity, the reality of their lives. My friendship with and admiration for the little Polish widow may have prompted my secret campaigns.

There was absolutely no way to give her anything like food to take out of the compound. The guards at the gate searched the Poles thoroughly both coming and going. Any contraband would be discovered at once. I resolved to take things out and give them to her somewhere else. It may have been the image of that little boy in her locket. I knew he was huddled somewhere out in the city, alone and hungry.

It was really quite simple. I would put a little food under my clothes and go shopping. Walking up to the guards at the gate, hiding my nervousness, I smiled cheerfully.

"Where are you going today, then, Klara?"

"Oh, guess what I'm cooking tonight?" I responded, and then described to them incredible visions of home-cooked German food. The Bielany cooking was horrible. The preparation of these fantastic dishes, I explained, required certain spices and extras which could only be found at a shop down the street from the compound. I told them in agonizing detail exactly what each spice would do for the food. Laughing and joking, they practically pushed me out the gate, food still hidden under my clothes.

I went to the shop in question. I walked around and looked at various things on counters and shelves. Finally the little widow opened the door and looked anxiously around the shop until she spotted me.

She never looked at me again, talking instead in Polish to the woman who ran the shop. I slipped a piece of bread wrapped in brown paper out of my blouse and put it carefully on a shelf when none of the other few customers were looking. Circulating around the store, I deposited a small sack of sugar and a sort of pancake of butter also wrapped in paper. Picking up a few herbs and spices as I went, I finally came to the woman in charge and paid her for my few purchases.

I hadn't seen the small, pale woman pick up any of the things I had deposited. We hadn't spoken or even looked at each other. Any of the other customers could be collaborating with our German intelligence. The shopkeeper almost certainly was "trusted" by the Germans, since she was allowed to operate so close to a secret

Klara

installation. As I headed for the door, though, I saw that the bread and butter were gone. The sugar was in a side aisle.

The guards were very interested in my herbs and spices when I returned. That evening, the men who had been on duty that day actually got to share in some of my results. That was an even bigger hit. Food like that could not be found anywhere in occupied Poland, they exclaimed.

Sharing this home cooking turned out to be a foolproof strategy. My mission to the shop was repeated many times over the following months. In time virtually every guard in camp looked forward eagerly to being on duty when I happened to want to make a trip for spices.

In spite of the austere, secretive atmosphere of the place, I was gradually carving out a little life for myself. I even made some tiny progress at swimming. I could actually let go of the edge of the pool and float awkwardly in the dark for brief periods. I never did it for long, though, because I was always afraid that in the dark I might float away from the edge of the pool. When I reached out it might be gone. It was that dark in the pool area. You could not see your hand in front of your face.

On the way out from the pool, walking through the long basement hallway to the stairs, we had to pass by the supply room where uniforms and other personal articles were issued. Another Otto worked there, not much like my brother except for the name. It would be fair to say he was crazy about my cooking. Otto was a big fellow.

One day as I was leaving the pool area after a swim, hair all wet and plastered against my head, I saw Otto was having an argument with a young man I didn't know, a noncommissioned officer. I hadn't seen him before in the compound.

"But these socks don't fit me! They're too big!"

Otto only looked at him.

"Here. Look at this." Exasperated and intense, he quickly bent down and pulled one of the socks on right over his shoes. It went on with no trouble, and there was room to spare inside.

"Look at that!" he commanded, pointing at his foot. "How can you say these socks are right for me?"

Otto just shrugged his shoulders. "Is it really that important? They'll work anyway, won't they? Just lace up the shoes, and the socks will be fine."

I came up as far as the doorway.

"Hello, Klara!" Otto called, winking.

The young man turned and looked at me. Who was interrupting his quest for socks that fit? His eyes were sharp as razors. He seemed to look straight through me. Though it hadn't started as anything, that glance suddenly took on a life of its own. He seemed to be looking past my eyes, straight into me. Shaking off this unexpected feeling, I turned toward Otto.

"What are you doing, Otto? Why are you causing such trouble?"

Otto only smiled. Everyone had their own little games to play. A newcomer had to expect a little bit of initiation.

"Come on now, Otto. Look at that sock," I said, pointing at the sock still hanging loosely about the shoe. "That is ridiculous!" I couldn't suppress a laugh.

The young stranger seemed embarrassed, caught in such an undignified pose. He took the sock off uncomfortably.

"Why don't you just give him socks that fit?" I asked. "I know you have every size of sock in the world in there, you rascal." Otto smiled even more broadly. That was fine with him.

"Since it's you asking, Klara, I'll do it," he said. "But next time you fix sauerbrauten, you have to promise to invite me!"

"I promise."

Otto positively grinned with glee, and turned to get the socks. The young man looked relieved.

"Thanks," he said.

"Oh, it's no trouble," I smiled. "He was just teasing you. I bet he would have given them to you in a minute anyway." I waved to Otto and went on my way back to the barracks.

As I was crossing the lawn, though, the young stranger caught up with me.

"Listen," he said, "I want to thank you again. That was very nice of you."

Klara

I turned to look at him, surprised he had followed. And suddenly there were those eyes again, darkest brown, piercing deep, seeming to look straight into my heart. I wondered if it were an illusion. Could he see or sense my feelings, my thoughts? I've never met anyone, before or since that day, with such piercing insight, such magnetism. He wasn't behaving oddly. He seemed perfectly normal, a nice young man, except for that incredible feeling of overpowering magnetism.

I must have said something foolish. I seemed to stumble mentally, to lose my balance somehow. But he smiled, and as we walked we struck up a very unusual conversation. His name, I learned, was Genya. He had just arrived at Bielany a day or two earlier. He was from Latvia.

I told him I was from the Ukraine, and that my roommate was from Latvia, too. Genya was astonished by this news. It made him very happy. Abruptly, he began to confide to me that he had a rough time getting along with "German" Germans. They treated him as a second class citizen because he was volksdeutsche, he said. He began to talk to me in Russian, refusing to go back to German. I went along with him, and spoke Russian too.

I told him how I had worked as a nurse. I even mentioned a little about my schooling in the Ukraine as a young girl. I don't know why I was telling him these things. We had only just met. In a curious way, I seemed to have lost control of my own actions while I was talking to him. His personality seemed to dominate us both, without any deliberate actions on his part. It was an alarming new feeling but it fascinated me. I had never met anyone like Genya before.

By the time I reached my barracks, I had agreed to join him after dinner and look over some of the Russian books he had with him. He offered to lend them to me if I wanted to read any of them.

Shortly after meeting Genya, as winter descended on us where we huddled on the banks of the Vistula, the stress of the cold and the war began to take their toll on me. I caught a cold. I didn't deal with it properly. I began to have dizzy spells and went to see the new doctor. He discovered I had phlebitis.

And so I found myself on a train riding back home to Germany on sick leave. Mama met me at the train. She showed me the telegram the Luftwaffe had sent ahead of me and looked very concerned about me. She cried over me and I cried over her, and we set out together up the hill to our house. On the way up the hill, she told me that Papa finally had been drafted into the army despite whatever suspicions the Nazis may have harbored about him. He now fought somewhere on the Russian front, just like Otto, she said. I saw the terrible, exhausted fear in her eyes as she said it.

The war had changed Melsungen, too. The land across the street from our house had been open meadow when I left, less than a year earlier. Only the row of new houses on our side, part of Hitler's building programs from the 1930s, had been there then.

Now there was evidence of another kind of building program. On the other side of the street, large grey barracks confronted me where only meadow had been. A few soldiers walked guard duty around them, cold and uncomfortable in the wintry weather.

I asked Mama what they were. She said that was where the Russian and Ukrainian and Polish laborers were housed. Penned into tiny rooms, they were taken out only for gang labor in town or in the neighboring countryside. Now the "background scenery" even in our little town had been changed, marred to match the changes in our own lives.

The whole mood of life was drastically different than it had been even a year before. Everyone knew, said Mama, these barracks were full of "slaves" who did all the dirty work in town. The guards were far from the pick of the German army. They beat the people in the camp. Some sold rations meant for prisoners on the black market. The blustery, proud, cheerful German spirit in the town had almost vanished. It was common to see a shadow, some secret shame or guilt, pass across faces. People shifted their eyes from side to side while you talked to them. The war, the way it was being conducted, did something very sad to the fabric of all our lives.

Resting at home, I spent a lot of time just talking to Mama. She seemed literally starved for conversation. That is how one day she came to ask me a question for which we had no answers.

"Klara, this labor camp is a bad place. But I've heard stories about worse things. I don't know what to think. Do you remember ten years ago, when we had just gotten here, how they began to chase out all the Jews?"

I nodded.

"Well, what has happened to them all, Klara? Where have they gone? Are they all gone to America? Are they all resettled in Poland and Russia?"

"I don't know."

"Nobody knows, Klara! That's what seems so strange to me. Germany has no place where they could send them, where people can just disappear. It isn't that big."

I couldn't explain it.

"I've heard stories, Klara," she said, more quietly now. "Terrible stories. Some people say we are locking up the Jews in huge prisons."

My mind leaped back to my first ride through Warsaw. But that had been an awful mistake, an isolated atrocity! Hadn't it? I wanted to believe that.

"We couldn't be doing such things, mamma. I can't believe it! It must be rumors started by the enemy. Probably it's English propaganda which spreads such stories. You mustn't ever repeat such things."

Neither of us felt we had resolved this enigma. But my mother shifted the conversation. She talked about the barracks across the street. Some prisoners were Russians. When they weren't working they sometimes had exercise periods. They could walk along the street under the eyes of not too vigilant guards. They had found out she spoke Russian, so sometimes they would casually stroll past the wooden fence when mother was working in the yard. They sometimes managed to get a potato or something from her, unnoticed, or simply a little Russian conversation. It was a small thing, but we knew how much it meant to them and also how serious it would be if mother's little "contacts" were discovered. Like my trips to the shop for spices, though, it offered a small way of fighting off a sense of helplessness which sprang from the inhumanity and drab ugliness the war was washing over our lives.

Then one morning, Mama and I were having breakfast peacefully in the kitchen. Suddenly a terrible commotion exploded in the street outside. Greatly disturbed at the screaming and shouting, I asked what was going on. Mama stepped to the window. She turned back to me, a tired look in her eyes.

"They're just beating them again."

At that point recklessness and stupidity triumphed even more completely. For some reason, the sound of screaming at breakfast just snapped something in me. I got up, rushed out the door. I could see a truck in the street with a few laborers inside, and a soldier and a young boy in the street itself. The boy couldn't have been more than twelve. He didn't even come up to the soldier's shoulder. The soldier was hitting him. The boy cringed, holding up his arms to ward off the blows.

Before I knew what I was doing I had run down the path, banged through the gate, and rushed onto the guard. I was still in my house robe. I was at him in an instant, yelling and clawing. Taken by surprise, he reeled away from the boy, who was as shocked as the guard. The people in the truck sat like plaster statues with mouths dropped open.

We all stopped, my momentum gone. For a moment we froze in this strange tableau. We all stared at each other in shocked silence. The enormity of what I had done began to filter into my awareness. My heart jumped into my mouth.

"You should be ashamed!" I yelled. "If the Fuhrer knew what you were doing, that you were beating this child, what would he do to you? I'm ashamed for you!"

That was all I could think of on the spur of the moment. Before he could say anything, or indeed recover from my onslaught, I wheeled about and ran back into the kitchen. Mama stood just inside the door, absolutely white. I sat, numb with dread, for the rest of the morning.

By some miracle nothing came of it. I never heard another word about it. Instead, shortly afterwards I was found to have recovered from my illness. I embarked for the journey back to my tiny world on the edge of occupied Warsaw.

Chapter Six
A TEARING OF THE HEART

By the time I got back from Melsungen, Germany was losing the war in earnest. The taut, lined face of the officer giving our weekly briefings betrayed the bad news, no matter what he was reading to us. We had captured Kharkov about the time I first came to Warsaw; I remember trying to picture German troops visiting the Kharkov Zoo on furlough as I had done on our passage out of Russia. Now the Russians had recaptured the city. We never heard this officially, but Hans confided to me that he had heard reports of Russian planes taking off and landing from bases west of Kharkov. There could be little doubt.

Erika and I took to sitting outside against the west wall of the barracks in the afternoon sun. It was about the only sunlight we could find for ourselves in that dreary season. From there we could continue our vigilant sentry duty on the entrance to the officers' quarters.

"Who visits Hans?" I asked one afternoon, as we sat in our accustomed spot.

"Oh, come on, Klara. You should know better."

"What do you mean?"

"Hans never invites other girls in there. He only has eyes for you. Why, it's almost comical."

"What!?"

"Don't play dumb with me. Anybody can see that."

Anybody except me, perhaps. I hadn't suspected a thing.

I knew he enjoyed my company. We spent many evenings together after our trip into the city, always in the compound after that. But to me we had been good friends and nothing more.

"He's a wonderful man, Klara! If he really is serious about you, just think how happy you could be with him after the war."

"Well, no one can tell what will happen to any of us after the war," I had to object. "Neither of us may survive. I don't think it's any use to start planning for after the war."

"Okay, maybe not. But think of now, then! He's such a wonderful man."

"You sound like you're in love with him yourself," I observed.

There was a pause in the conversation. I looked over at Erika quickly. She was being uncommonly still. Had I stepped on another hidden land mine?

"Are you in love with him, Erika?"

"Oh, Klara, don't be stupid!" she blurted out in frustration, avoiding my eyes. "How could I know a thing like that? I've never even been with him for an evening. I've barely even talked to him."

She was crazy about him. She thought he was crazy about me. We were closest friends. Did such things really happen to people? I had to wonder. I knew I would have to find out where the truth lay before long.

My opportunity came sooner than I might have wished. It was only a night or so later. I left the cafeteria, pulling on my winter coat, and went for a stroll with Hans after dinner. Together we wandered down the long gentle hillside behind the main building. Far below us, faint in the gathering dusk, I could just glimpse outlines of the distant munitions dump. Above and behind us the shadowy bulk of the main building jutted up from a crust of snow on the ground.

"It's not a good sign, Klara," Hans was saying. "We send out what we know of the movements of Russian planes. The fighters have plenty of time. But we never seem to shoot down as many as we did last year."

"Maybe the Russians are getting to be better pilots?"

"Oh, perhaps. But they seem to have more planes, too. Always another flight of Russian planes to worry about. Some spotter plane of theirs sees our every move. And we don't have as many planes as we did this time last year! Not in the air, anyway."

We stopped. I looked at him.

"Are we losing the war?"

Perhaps I shouldn't have asked that question. He might have reported such questions to the higher-ups. I didn't think so, or I never would have asked. What I didn't consider was that he might suspect the same of me. He gave me a long, quizzical look before he replied.

Klara

"We most certainly are losing. Every day the Russians get stronger and we lose our own strength. I wonder if we can ever mount another offensive."

He stepped closer to me.

"Klara, I can't tell what will happen any more than you can. I hope for the best, that's all." There was a pause. I remained quiet. "I hope for a lot of time with you, Klara."

How right had Erika been?

"We already have had a lot of time together, Hans."

He put his arm around my shoulder and drew me to his side as we walked on slowly. "I know. So far, so good."

I tried to think of something incisive to say, something to get him to reveal where his feelings lay, where this conversation might be going.

"I think your judgement is a little clouded in this place," I said at last. "There are only twelve of us women here, and look at all of you men!"

"As far as I'm concerned, there aren't even twelve," he replied. "There is only one."

Good Lord. Erika was right.

"Erika is crazy about you, Hans," I said quietly, after casting about in a sort of panic for some way to get the conversation under control again.

He was silent for many paces after that. We didn't stop walking; to stop would have created such an awkward situation that the whole conversation would have collapsed. Neither of us wanted it to collapse.

"And you?" he said, after that enormous silence.

"I don't know, Hans," I answered honestly. "My judgement is clouded too."

"Is there someone else at home?"

"No."

Was that the truth? It seemed like the truth that evening.

"There are just so many of you to choose from!" I told him, smiling, trying to break the heavy seriousness of the discussion. It was beginning to frighten me. Another minute and he would have been asking me to marry him.

He took a minute to digest this hint on my part. Finally he accepted the change in the weather.

"Aha!" he laughed. "We shall have to begin a lottery system. We men will choose numbers, and you women will each get a hat with two dozen or so numbers to choose from. That way we will all have a sporting chance, anyway!"

I laughed gratefully. We finished our walk in a lighter mood.

But Erika had been right about Hans. How did I really feel about that? It was hard for me to decide. I couldn't tell him because I didn't know the answer in my own heart. Certainly there was no hint of any feeling such as I had known with Rudi. Was I doomed to a life of pale comparisons with that first love?

I couldn't exist long in that lonely condition, trying to guess at such imponderables. I decided I would have to talk to Erika no matter how it might come out.

I saw my chance a few nights later. We were getting ready to go to sleep. Erika had just finished telling me about a morbid dream she had suffered though.

"I dreamed I was dying again," she complained. This was not the first such dream for her. "It was terrible. I wish it would stop."

"Erika," I began, changing the subject.

"Hmmm?" Her back was to me, her voice muffled by the sweater she was trying to pull over her head.

"I had a long talk with Hans the other night."

She finished taking off the sweater more quickly, and turning, sat down on her bed and looked at me attentively.

"About what?"

"You told me he was crazy about me," I reminded her.

"He is."

"I think you're right, Erika," I said. She looked at me sharply.

"Why do you say that? It must have been some conversation!"

"He told me he hoped he would get to spend a lot of time with me," I answered.

"That sounds like the beginning of a proposal if I ever heard one."

"I know. I thought so, too. So I changed the subject."

Erika laughed a little. "What did you talk about, the weather or the war?"

Here goes, I thought. "We talked about you," I said. "I told him you were crazy about him."

She just looked at me for a minute.

"Me!?"

I nodded quietly, waiting for her to continue. A pained expression crossed her face. With a sigh of exasperation she looked down at the bedclothes beside her. "Oh, Klara, why did you have to say a stupid thing like that?"

"You just said he was getting ready to propose, Erika. And I don't love him."

She looked at me again quickly.

"And you do, Erika. Don't you!?" I demanded.

She was silent for a moment. At last she lowered her eyes.

"I guess I do, Klara. I know I told you there are lots of women here who are crazy about him, but with me I think it's different. I don't think I'll ever meet anyone like him again."

"Don't you start with your stories about how you're going to die again!" I warned. That got a smile from her.

"Klara, you're a good friend. But why did you have to tell him that I love him? I'll never be able to look him in the eye again! What a fool he must think I am!"

"For loving him? He should think you're a woman of good taste!" I countered. We both laughed out loud. Erika moved over to my bed and gave me a big hug.

"Well," she decided, "he may never take me seriously anyway. But at least now he knows about my side of the situation."

"And he won't be thinking of marrying me any longer, I don't think," I added. "Maybe he'll come to his senses now."

We talked late into that night. Not wanting to dwell on the awkward issue of her future with Hans, Erika soon changed the course of our conversation. It would be fine if Hans came to his senses, she agreed, but what about me? When did I plan to come to mine? Not only didn't I appreciate Hans, but she thought I was seeing far too much of Genya.

Genya and Erika had met soon after my first encounter with him. In fact I had engineered that first meeting. I thought perhaps since they were both from Latvia they might have hit it off. That would have been another way of resolving the triangle of Hans, Erika and myself. But things had not exactly worked out as I had intended.

"What do you see in him?" Erika asked me now. "He's an odd one."

"What's so odd about him?" I said defensively.

"He's so moody," she complained. "He always wants to talk so seriously. About such weighty things." This seemed strange coming from the same Erika who began my political education, but she didn't see anything in the comparison.

"We're not alike at all!" she insisted. "And you had no business playing matchmaker, trying to set us up together. Oh, yes you did! Anyway, there's no point in that, because it's clear this one is stuck on you, too. What is it with you? Some kind of secret perfume?"

Even I could see she was right about that. Genya was very attached to me. Though it was difficult to use that word in connection with him. He seemed to dominate any gathering simply by the force of his personality, by his mere presence. It was an intangible but real power --you could almost feel it in the air.

And he did like to talk about serious things. Before we had known each other a month he had told me all about his childhood. His father had owned a large furniture factory in Riga. They had been very wealthy. He recounted childhood memories of piano lessons, and grand vacations, and lots of servants in a mansion of a house. Quite different from the farm where I had grown up! I didn't stress my background much.

His father, I also learned, had run off with the family's young blonde maid. Genya was only a little boy when it happened. The incident hurt him deeply. Perhaps that partly accounted for why he was so driven, so intense. He seemed to spend his days in a "trajectory," trying to go somewhere. He pursued an intangible future, one he could never reach. He was running away from his past, his family, perhaps even himself.

Knowing such things about him after only a few days of our acquaintance, it wasn't a total surprise to learn he already had volunteered to parachute behind Russian lines.

"Are you crazy!?" I objected. "You're practically guaranteed to be captured and killed outright!"

He didn't deny it. But from his point of view it made a kind of sense. He wanted change. It was time to do something dangerous and incredible, to prove he was as German as anybody else in the Reich. There was an element of fanaticism in his plans but after all, as I had warned Erika, who knew whether they would survive the war anyway?

Still, parachuting behind Russian lines was a bit much. I talked him into withdrawing his name for that assignment. He told me he had done it because at the time, he had nothing to live for. Now he did, he said, meaning me. Erika was right again.

But this was different. I could look Hans in the eye and admit to myself he was a wonderful man, but I was perfectly clear that I didn't love him. He was fun. He was nice. He would make a wonderful husband, but not for me.

And Genya?

Perhaps it was the tension of the war, the isolation there at Bielany, or simply Genya's eyes. Whatever the reason, I had a strange, indescribable feeling about him. It wasn't the same sort of feeling I had for Rudi, in that fairytale springtime now fading into the past. That, I told myself, wasn't necessarily bad. The same feeling might have produced the same conclusion.

I did find myself attracted to Genya. Actually, mesmerized by him would have been closer to the mark. Other people felt the same uncanny power of his personality, but not the way it affected me.

This feeling, sometimes a little alarming, wasn't actually unpleasant. I really enjoyed his company. He was very polite and charming, a true old world aristocrat at heart. With his sparkling sense of humor, almost any topic under the sun made for fascinating conversation. Once we sat at dinner in the cafeteria in the evening, just the two of us left at our table. Suddenly he began talking about politics.

"Did I ever tell you I was a communist once?" he smiled, quietly.

Though I was used to the unlikely things he could bring up, this caught me by surprise. He had to laugh at my amazed expression. "I was still in gimnazium," he explained, leaning forward. "I must have been about twelve or thirteen. I had the books hidden under my bed at home. If my teachers had found out! But you know what I mean. You got such material right in the schoolroom."

I nodded. We could talk to each other about the power of communist propaganda on a young mind. That shared background meant more to us both, I think, than we realized at the time.

"Oh, they had me convinced!" he went on. "I thought the revolution was the most wonderful thing that had ever happened in the history of the world. Didn't you ever feel like that, too?"

"I wrote an essay once," I replied. "My teacher liked it so much he entered it in a competition. He said my clear thinking was just what the revolution needed." I thought back to Comrade Plotsky for the first time in years.

Genya nodded. "So what happened?"

"To the essay?"

"No, to your communism."

"We left Russia," I said simply. Again he nodded. We seemed to feel precisely the same memories, to understand exactly what the other person meant.

"And you?" I went on.

"Well, I think I changed even before we left. I think it was the Latvian movement that changed me."

I knew he had gotten caught up in the fierce patriotism of that little nation, which only existed for a brief time between the two world wars. He did not leave Latvia until the Russians took control in 1938.

"They marched in, and I fled the country." He made a face, clearly still feeling the bitterness of that experience. "So then I joined the German Luftwaffe."

I smiled. "I joined the Girls' Hitler Youth so I could have the uniform," I admitted.

"You know, Klara," he said then, "we're very different people. You're so calm, so peaceful--" I started to protest. "--no, you really are. And I'm too emotional. But in another way we really are very much alike. I think we understand each other, you and I."

I had to nod my head at that. We did understand each other.

"I know there are other men here at Bielany interested in you, Klara," he went on. "Please don't be upset at what I want to say." He moved closer. "Klara, it's more than understanding. I love you."

I looked steadily into his eyes. We really did understand each other. Just as he could look straight into my heart, I suddenly realized I could look straight into his.

"Genya, I'm not involved with other men here at Bielany," I said at last. "I had no idea at first, but I believe I love you too."

Had I said that?

I tried to reach back, to catch my words and listen to them once more. I had said it. My feelings were much different from the way I had felt when pushing Rudi in his wheelchair. Calling both feelings "love" was too simple. But I realized at last that in a new and different way I was in love with Genya, too.

About the time I became clearly aware that things had come to this, he was shipped out to someplace around Minsk.

The Russians had been advancing like a prairie fire. Particularly in the south, across the Ukraine, they rolled up German armies like an old dusty rug. Early in November they captured Kiev, the western twin to Kharkov which I had never seen but had always heard so much about. Assignment to the vicinity of Minsk meant he was practically at the front!

We had a very intense goodbye. He kissed me that day for the first time. The experience shocked us both, I think. It was like an electric spark, as when one accidentally comes in contact with a live electric wire.

He was posted to an advanced listening station, very hazardous duty. Not only was he at the front, he was in front of the front. Out ahead of the main line of defensive positions, the German army stationed isolated radio listening posts at intervals along the front. Their mission was to eavesdrop on enemy radio communication, to intercept coded and uncoded messages and obtain independent directional fixes on transmissions. Observations from different stations could be used to triangulate and locate enemy transmitters, giving the positions of headquarters, airfields, columns of troops, and the like.

After he left we couldn't communicate much at all. I told myself that when he left, I would find out how I truly felt about him. Perhaps the whole thing depended on his unusual presence, so once he was physically absent the whole business would fall flat?

It did not. I missed him very much. I worried about his safety. Was this love? Whatever it was, I felt it.

Genya felt it, too. He came back on a two-day pass early in January of 1944, as the winter raged about us. We spent nearly every hour of that leave together when I was not on duty.

On the afternoon of the second day of his pass we went for a walk on the same long, bare hillside where Hans and I had come to our understanding. This time it was a freezing cold winter day, but with a hard blue sky above and plenty of snow underfoot. Bundled up as we were, there was not a lot of hugging and kissing, but it was a momentous walk.

"I have a terrible amount of time to think when I'm alone in my little listening post," he told me. "And you know what I think about the most?" He looked over at me. I shook my head. Our breath came out like smoke.

"I think about Russian soldiers creeping toward me in the snow. I think about getting killed."

"You sound like Erika. But everybody must think about getting killed. I could be killed by partisans when I go out shopping to the market."

"I know, I know. But there really is a high risk I may be killed, and I don't want that to happen before I achieve something in life."

"And what is that?"

He turned to stand in front of me suddenly.

Klara

"To marry you, Klara. What if I get killed before I can marry you?" He was not joking. His face was worried, not laughing. Of all the times I was at a loss for words, this took first prize easily.

There was a pause, and then he asked "Will you marry me, Klara?"

We stood there on that snowy hillside on the north edge of occupied Warsaw. On the edge of a wholly new direction in our lives.

When he left again, we were engaged to be married.

I still don't know how that happened. It was a blur in my mind, even at the time. I remember I was a little stunned by the fact myself, the next day when I told Erika.

"You must be crazy," she said flatly. "He's an oddball! I can't for the life of me understand why you like him at all." Erika was not a master of tact. She cared for me, though, and she thought I was making a big mistake. She told me so. In fact, the warnings seemed to come from every side. As a rule the officers in the listening room never bothered with me. Only one older Luftwaffe officer took me under his wing. He decided to watch out for me among all those men because he had a daughter about my age, and I reminded him of her. When he learned about my engagement to Genya through the grapevine, one day he drew me aside as I was coming on duty.

"Klara, I heard about your plans to get married." He wasn't congratulating me. "Listen, my dear. I don't mean to meddle, but are you perfectly sure you are doing the right thing?"

I wasn't quite sure how to respond. "Why do you ask, sir?"

He, too, described Genya as a loner, an unusual person. He seemed concerned about my decision.

But after all, none of them were engaged to Genya. I was. I had no doubts in my mind. Perhaps I wanted to bring him out of his shell and make him a happier, friendlier person. I knew the warmth and imagination inside him, and wished he could share that with more people. To be honest, I was still in search of a "mission" in life. Perhaps he was it.

The winter of 1943-44 finally came to an end. No one could escape from the fact anymore that Germany was losing very badly on the Russian front. Such admissions still never occurred in official briefings, but we all knew that nearly all of Russia proper had been recaptured by the Red Army. Then as 1944 began to grind out its course, Stalin's juggernaut gradually flooded across southeastern Europe. Poland, however, we defended furiously. It was the last buffer before German territory. Now the front was very much closer to us. Minsk was in Russian hands.

This meant I got to see Genya more often, though, so even in the midst of defeat I was able to find some good news.

In fact, life still went on pretty much as it had in 1943 when I first arrived. I still made an occasional trip to the Polish shop with my little secret items for the widow. Erika and I still kept tabs on the officers' quarters. In fact, a couple of times I saw Erika herself going into that building with Hans! Our work, our meals, everything kept on in defeat as it had in victory. Even our swimming periods continued, until suddenly an unexpected tragedy struck from that quarter.

It was an unusually warm day in late April or early May, and everyone felt hot and tired. We trooped down into the basement, changed into our suits in the absolute darkness of the pool area, and put our clothes along the wall in a prearranged order so we could find them again.

Then, laughing and calling to each other in the dark, we ran across the cold floor toward the edge of the pool. The girl who changed the fastest announced triumphantly, "I win!" I heard the slap of her feet as she ran across to the pool. One or two more pairs of footfalls started after her. We heard her leap onto the diving board. We heard the board spring back as she made her graceful dive.

But instead of a small splash, the darkness was pierced by her shriek and then a dull thump, not that loud but clear for all of us to hear. The pool was empty. No one had told us. She smashed headfirst into the concrete bottom and was killed instantly; she never even had time to finish her cry.

All of the rest of us who were there were frozen in our tracks, the horrifying sounds of her fall echoing in our ears in the cool

Klara

darkness. Every heart in the room must have stopped beating for a moment.

We didn't go down into the dry pool. We only ran out to the guards at the front desk. They called the hospital. As we ran through the hall in the basement, wild with panic and the horror of what had happened, all at once I saw Erika running ahead of me in her white bathing suit. So this had not been the death she had been fearing, either. I remember thinking that perhaps dreams aren't much to worry about, after all.

None of us went down to that pool to swim again. It would have been an exercise in horror to swim in that dark, cold water, unable to see anything, thinking all the time about the smashed body of our friend in the bottom of that pool.

The memory of this grisly episode had not faded far from our daily lives when on a Friday in mid-May I went to Melsungen to prepare for my wedding. Genya was to follow the next day from the front. We both had managed by some miracle to get leave.

As Otto was still away, Genya stayed in his room at our house. My mother went to the old Lutheran church and talked with the minister about the service. He arranged for Genya and me to come to his home the day before the wedding to record some information. He and I were still very close, ever since confirmation days. I had talked and prayed with him about my survival of the Kassel bombing. He had agreed with Mama that God had given me a special gift of survival in the midst of the war.

That evening my mother came up to my room to talk to me.

"Klara, I honestly don't know what I should do with this." She had an envelope in her hand. "It came in the mail for you about four or five days ago. I thought about giving it to you after the wedding, but that would be even more out of place. So here. You better see what you want to do with it."

She left again. I glanced at the letter she left on my bed. It was from Mainz. It was from Rudi.

I stared at the letter.

I don't know how long I did nothing but stare at it, but at last I picked it up. It had not been opened. It was not a long letter, I could tell, because the envelope felt light in my hand. It was beautiful stationery.

I felt confusion, sitting there on the eve of my wedding holding a letter from another man, a man I had loved passionately in another time. I felt I was doing something wrong. Yet at the same time I didn't believe that. I opened the letter.

"Dear Klara," it read. "It has been long years since I wrote to you. We were both younger then, and neither of us could know our minds truly. Though I have not written to you in all these years, I have thought of you constantly."

I could almost see him again, hear him saying the words.

"The doctors at Davos brought me through, just as they said they could. It took two and a half years, but they did it. I made a complete recovery. The tuberculosis is gone."

My heart was glad at that news.

"I am working in a hospital here in Mainz as an intern. We are working with floods of wounded men from the front. My surgical training is going rapidly. My internship will be completed before the end of the year."

So he was going to be a surgeon, just as he had always dreamed.

"Klara, I still love you with all my heart! I almost convinced myself our future could not be, while I lay in that bed in Davos. But I never stopped loving you. I have not seen you for several years, but I know you are still the same. I know you are more beautiful than ever. I still love you more than ever. When I am in practice for myself, my parents cannot tell me what to do. I will not let them stand between us. Will you please write back to me? Tell me you still love me! Tell me you will wait for me, and that you will see me at Christmas! Do you remember I said I would be back for you by Christmas? I did not come that year. I will come this year! We will be one at last! I love you. Rudi."

It was all fitted onto the front and back of a single sheet of white linen writing paper. Until I turned it over to read the back, I had no warning of what was coming. There was a beautiful photograph of him, too.

Klara

I lay dazed on the bed for a long time, the letter dangling in my hand. My mind whirled aimlessly, desperately, without forming any coherent thoughts about anything. How could this be!?

After what seemed like an eternity of confusion, I found myself getting up from the bed and opening my dresser. There in the drawer was the dusty stack of letters we had written to each other years before, tied neatly with string. There was a little white card on top of the stack, with the crumbling remains of a little white flower still fastened to it--Edelweiss.

Ever so gently, I took out that little card and stood holding it. What am I going to do? What can I do? What can I do? I trembled so, I almost dropped the petals off the card. I had to put it down on the dresser again. I turned this way and that, twisting my hands in futile gestures of confusion.

At last I got down on my knees beside the bed and prayed. Please God, I pleaded, help me in this hour of trouble! Give me peace in my heart. Give me the strength to know what to do! I ran over the words in my mind several times, before I felt I had done as much as I could. Then I went to my window and looked out over the town absently.

And after a time, I knew. I knew my heart, I knew my future. Then I picked up his letter, the little white card, and the stack of old love letters. Slowly, I walked down the stairs to the living room before my will could fail me.

Our little stove still had a bed of red coals glowing in it, for the nights were still chilly in May. I opened the stove and stood looking into the fiery red glow for a while.

Then I slowly dropped Rudi's last letter in. It lay there a moment. Suddenly bright yellow flames burst about it and it was gone. The light streamed up from the stove, sending a giant shadow of my head and arms dancing about the wall and ceiling behind me. I untied the string, and one by one, fed the other letters into the flames.

Finally I was standing there in the dark again, the last letter gone, holding only the little white card. I looked at the dried, crumbling blossom. "Ever faithful," it meant. I held it thus for a long moment. I closed my eyes and dropped it in the fire.

I looked down then, quickly, in time to see the card go brown all over at once and then shrivel and burn away. The fragile dried flower was consumed in an instant, so quickly I could not really even see it burn.

All was gone. The image of the card, the little flower in the midst of the flames, still burned in my eyes as I walked numbly back up the stairs to my room. I cried quietly into my old, forgiving feather quilt. I saw the delicate flower in my dreams.

The next day was my wedding day, and I knew what I had to do. I got married to Genya. It was the only choice I really had, and I loved him. My mother, my aunt Josephine, and my sister Aline were the only guests.

After the wedding, my mother and aunt prepared the best feast one could muster in a country that was rapidly losing a war. Aunt Josephine had slaughtered and brought along a rooster for our delicious soup. After dinner we sat talking for a long time.

Genya and I left the next day, Monday. I went back to Warsaw, and he went back to his post at the front. My life in Bielany resumed. My life had changed so much I hardly recognized myself in the mirror. It couldn't have been more than a day or two after I returned that Erika came triumphantly into the room.

"Look at this, Klara!" she exclaimed. She had a letter. "It's from my parents!"

"In Riga?" I asked.

"No! They've been living in Dresden for four months already! They began planning to leave almost right away after the Germans entered Latvia, and this past spring they actually packed up and moved back to Dresden. Isn't that wonderful?"

I had to agree that was the best news we had heard in some time. Now her family was safe in a German city, well out of the fighting.

A day or two later, as if in celebration of the good news, Erika witnessed another miracle. We hadn't seen so much as a morsel of meat in our rations at Bielany for weeks and weeks. Something had happened to the supplies. Then one day Erika came running in.

"Klara! Come quick! The trucks are here. There's meat on them!"

Klara

I had to go to work, but she told me to come straight to the cafeteria afterwards. When I finally got there I found she had gotten a whole box of frozen ground beef and made it into a fantastic dish of meatballs. She had invited all the women in the barracks to come to a little dinner at a table at the end of the room. We all agreed the meat was delicious!

It was also contaminated. Probably it had been too long in shipment. It may have gotten thawed and refrozen at some point.

Within less than an hour after eating, several of us began to get horrible cramps. I was actually lying on the floor in my room, in a knot in a corner moaning. Erika was beginning to feel the symptoms as well. Maybe she'll die right here this evening, I remember thinking. In fact, maybe so will I. Maybe her premonitions were right.

Erika had other ideas. She got a big bottle of vodka and forced me to join her in drinking great mouthfuls of it. We swallowed and swallowed. The horrible stuff burned like lava from a volcano in my throat. I thought my stomach was on fire. Still she made me drink more. We went outside, hearing groaning and moaning in other rooms. Just about the time we got to our little station on the west side of the building, the vodka hit us like a safe dropped from the peak of the barracks roof onto our heads.

I reeled. I was dizzy and nauseous.

"I think I'm going to be sick," I cried weakly.

"That's the idea!" Erika shot back. "Here, have another drink."

She refused to be put off. We drank the last of the bottle together. A whole bottle of vodka! Half in me, half in her. We vomited like crazy. The vodka came rushing back up. So did the bad meat. I felt so awful the next day that I was actually late for work.

But one of the other girls actually died from that meat. Poisoned. The guilt this inflicted on Erika was terrible to see. No one blamed her, for she had really been sharing a wonderful treat with us. She could have left the meat to be fed to everyone, and perhaps more would have died, or perhaps if it had been shared out among many, no one would actually have died. A paradox for all of us, a disaster for her. For a couple of months after that she could only do her job and go to the room to sit or sleep. She didn't talk much.

There was nothing I or anyone else could say about it that would help.

Chapter Seven
COLLAPSE AND FLIGHT

The radio conversations in my headphones made the unbelievably ferocious fighting along the Polish border seem practically outside the door of the listening room. Russia waxed stronger with each passing day. Still, somehow German armies held on. Instead of a rout, the Russian advance was kilometer by kilometer, at a fearful cost in lives to both sides. It was a bloody summer and fall.

But advance they did. It seemed inevitable that Warsaw would fall to the Red Army, as Bucharest and other Balkan capitals had done already. We knew we were doomed, that the end of the war was approaching. Our briefings still painted a picture of secret weapons, surprise offensives, and other unbelievable miracles, but no one could take such things seriously.

In good flying weather, Russian radio traffic swamped our little office. We always seemed to hear about their attacks against us, not our attacks against them. In the privacy of our room in the evenings, Erika and I pondered what might happen when Russian troops actually were crossing the Vistula, capturing Warsaw. Would we still sit in Bielany, we wondered, pretending we were about to take the offensive again?

Then in a massive winter offensive, the Russians suddenly surged forward toward Warsaw itself. That changed the atmosphere at Bielany entirely. That week there was no briefing. Soviet armored spearheads drove toward the capital. A German defensive line tried desperately to reform along the Vistula, but that river ran right through the middle of Warsaw, within easy artillery range (not to say rifle range!) of the Bielany compound itself. The front had dissolved. Our forward listening posts disappeared, every man for himself. I heard nothing about Genya. Was he alive? Had he been captured? There was no way to find out.

Warsaw tingled in every nerve. From Erika I heard that the Polish underground was stirring ominously in the city. Something like panic reigned among the Germans, and Bielany was not spared. Our top secret Luftwaffe command center had become much too vulnerable. Something had to be done.

And so one morning we woke up to a blood-chilling discovery. All the officers were gone! No notices, no briefing, no plan of evacuation. During the night, secret orders issued on a moment's notice had circulated among the "important" personnel. They quietly packed up and disappeared into the night. Only the less important people, chiefly enlisted men and the women in our women's barracks, were left behind.

We were on our own, abandoned by the Luftwaffe to survive as best we could. No transportation, no orders, nothing. Probably they had not been able to find transportation for all of us, leading to this callous triage in the night. The first day after the evaporation of Bielany was a curious one. There was no one left to give any orders, no jobs to do.

We stayed in our rooms nervously discussing the situation until nearly noon. Then Erika and I walked over to the cafeteria. Outside the windows we could see a steady trickle of people walking out the main gate, heading for the streetcar line and the central train station. I could just imagine the scene in that station at that moment. Probably we could not even have gotten inside the station doors.

A few enlisted men still maintained some semblance of order in the camp. Two guards stayed at the gate, writing down names of everyone as they left. It was reassuring to know at least the gates were secure, but this was a false sense of security.

Late in the afternoon, back in the barracks, a girl entered and paused to clap her arms together, pounding the icy outdoor cold out of her clothes. "Klara?" she called. I answered and she came in. "There's a Polish woman in the cafeteria looking for you," she related. "She's one of those who works over there."

Erika and I seized our coats, pausing only to button them up to our chins before we hurried across to the cafeteria building. As we stepped through the door I saw the small, pale china doll widow of the Polish officer standing just inside. She waved to us as we came in.

"I'm glad you're still here," she began, as we sat down. "I don't think you can get out of the city through the train station like everyone is trying."

Erika and I glanced at each other.

"How could they have just left all of you here like this?" the little widow continued. "The underground is moving. The uprising is already starting! I think your only hope now is to come with me. I can hide you from the Russians. It will be only a few days before they enter the city."

"We're together," I replied simply, gesturing toward Erika.

She considered a moment. "Two would not be much more difficult to hide than one," she decided. "But we must go quickly."

Erika and I looked at each other again. This was a riddle indeed.

"May we talk about this?"

"Of course, but you must be quick. I must leave again at once."

Erika and I moved to a corner of the room.

"Suppose we do it," I speculated. "What then? We find ourselves hiding in some attic in Warsaw?"

"While the war marches away to the west," Erika said doubtfully. "And leaves us in the middle of an ocean of Russian soldiers. And that is, if she is able to hide us! Who is to say we won't be discovered?"

I had a darker thought. "Does she mean what she says? Suppose this is a way for the underground to take hostages?"

We both glanced at her quickly. She stood with her back to us, looking out the window. The pose made her seem distant, a closed book. I didn't really think the little widow would repay my kindness with such a fate, but we were dealing in incalculable emotions now. Nothing was certain.

"She's your friend, Klara."

Erika's words turned me back to her. "I don't think I want to go," I finally decided. But was it the right choice? No way to know! Erika nodded. A few fateful steps carried me to the small woman's side. I gave her the news. She looked at me for a long moment, but I couldn't make out her expression. Was it pity, or relief, or sadness? Was she hurt that we didn't trust her? Then she got up and departed quickly, without another word. We sat down and had another cup of "coffee". Erika put a little vodka in it.

The evening and cold, windy night which followed held little sleep for the handful of us still hiding at Bielany, and even less peace of mind. A cold feeling in the pit of my stomach chilled me far more than the winter wind whistling outside the walls. More than once that night, Erika or I wondered aloud if we had been foolish to refuse the Polish widow's offer.

When morning dawned, pale and dreary, the fear intensified. One of the guards took a telephone call from the center of the city, warning him to be alert for signs of trouble. Fighting had broken out at key installations in the city, the radio station and the old parliament building and a dozen other places. The Warsaw Uprising was underway. And we were still trapped in Warsaw!

Erika and I descended into a mild panic. There was no point trying to go anywhere. There was nowhere to run. What was to become of us? We went to our room and sat on the bed, looking at a couple of bags we had been trying to pack, saying very little.

Suddenly, about eleven in the morning, the roar of a motor intruded from out on the road running past the camp. We rushed outside to join the few other holdouts still left behind.

A large German armored car! Swerving in through the gate, it clattered to a halt in the middle of the snow covered lawn. Our guard swung the gate closed and hurried after it. A Wehrmacht soldier got out, followed by another, and then a man in Luftwaffe blue.

It was Genya! He jumped down from the hatch on the top, dropped to the ground, and stood looking at me. He broke into a run and we rushed into each other's arms. He felt warm and sweaty against me in the chilly morning air. His clothes smelled of machine oil and the inside of the armored car. It was a wonderful smell. We just hugged each other tight for a minute. Not a word was said. None was needed.

Finally he drew back from me. "We've got to get out of Warsaw," he declared. "The whole city is a madhouse! By tomorrow there could be Russian troops right here in the street."

It was a dire situation. The tension was palpable. The few of us now remaining at Bielany quickly ate lunch with the soldiers. We sat around them as they wolfed down the little food we could offer, ravenous after days at the front with little or no supplies.

"It was terrible," said one of the Wehrmacht men, talking as he chewed. "The whole front was just collapsing everywhere. All the roads are full of men and equipment trying to retreat. The columns stretch on forever. They've gotten all jammed up; nobody seems to be able to move."

"We just took off across country," explained Genya. "We drove through streams and everything, and all the time we could see these long columns of people marching along all the roads in sight." He took a huge bite from the stale bread I had given him and washed it down with some thin soup in a big tin cup. "If I hadn't stood in the road in front of these guys and made them stop, I'd still be back there facing the Russian tanks!"

Then we all piled onto the armored car. Erika and I crawled down through the hatch and rode inside with the two crewmen and Genya. It was so cramped we could hardly move, except the driver who sat down below and in front of us in his own little seat. Five guards rode on the back of the car behind the little turret, helmets on and guns in their hands. Some other people rode up there with them on the outside. Genya directed the driver, who wasn't familiar with Warsaw, and we drove slowly out of the compound and down the street toward the city.

I couldn't see much from inside the car, but I heard scattered shooting off to one side or the other from time to time. We headed for the train station, to get everyone onto a train if the station was still in German hands. But before we got to the center of the city, we ran smack into the Uprising itself.

"There's a barricade across the street ahead," said Genya. "I see German soldiers."

"What about the Poles?" called the driver, without turning around. He slowed the car to a crawl.

"I think they must be in the houses between us and the barricade," Genya replied. "Polish snipers and partisans. I can hear the firing." We all could hear it. The car sat motionless in the side street, motor idling.

"We can't just sit here," the driver said. "I'll try to go around some other way."

We managed to thread our way through the chaotic maze of streets, closer and closer to the train station. Finally Genya advised the driver, "The train station is ahead and to the left several blocks."

"We can't do it," came the reply from the driver. "There's more barricades down those side streets all along here. I'm not going into that nest."

We all argued for a few moments, but the driver and his comrade wouldn't budge. They wanted to just get out of the city as fast as they could, in the armored car instead of a train. The guards and the others riding on top decided to jump off, and to try to find a way into the train station. Erika and I, though, stayed inside the car with Genya and the other two soldiers. We headed for the southwestern edge of the city.

I spent most of the trip on the floor, listening to the wheels humming on the roads below us. I did shift positions once or twice in a way that let me look out through a narrow viewport. The fragments of Warsaw I glimpsed were horrifying. Dead horses, dead people, wounded men, blinded, even legless, lay along the streets screaming for help. Carts loaded with possessions often ended as heaps of scattered debris, carts for which some Germans had paid a fortune in the panic of the retreat. Now they were upended and burning, dead bodies lying nearby on the street. The shooting and screaming never seemed to stop, a constant barrage of the most terrifying noises imaginable. I tried to shrink inside myself and disappear.

At last we got clear of the city, though. By some miracle, we had escaped in the midst of the Uprising. The car roared alone across the silent, frozen Polish countryside. We didn't even stop when it got dark, driving on and on through the night. At long last, sometime the next morning, we came to a halt. I had no idea where we were, but it was somewhere in the country, far from the city.

Genya got out of the vehicle with Erika and myself.

"We have to keep moving," he said. "But we are away from the front lines now. We crossed into Germany during the night, and there's a town with a train station just over there." He pointed off across some fields. "You go and catch a train and get back home!"

"What about you?" I asked, looking into his eyes,

"I'm going with them," he replied, gesturing back at the armored car. "We took off in this thing, and we have to stick with it now; we're not where we are supposed to be."

Klara

I understood. They had run away from the front. Deserters were shot on the spot; they couldn't risk wandering about in train stations. He hugged me goodbye, climbed back up into the car, and that was all. It drove away and left us standing alone on a small dirt track beside the fields.

Far behind us, on the edge of Warsaw, the Russians halted their advance. German generals caught their breath, saw this fact, and launched a crushing counterattack against the Warsaw Uprising. In the ensuing bloodbath I doubt that Erika and I would have survived, no matter what the little Polish widow's intentions.

Erika and I stumbled across the frozen terrain and eventually came to a farmhouse. The German family that lived there was very kind, but too afraid to take us in. They pointed us in the direction of the town with its small train station. Eventually we boarded a train headed in the direction of Dresden. I remember that train seemed to travel very fast. The cars shook and rattled and rocked alarmingly from side to side. There was nothing to eat, and it almost never stopped as we pushed onward.

We were rushing across open country, dotted with patches of forest here and there, when suddenly the train began to slow down. No one knew what was going on at first. Eventually, though, word filtered back through the cars that repairs to tracks ahead were behind schedule. Damage from a bombing raid was supposed to have been all cleared up in time for this train to pass, but it had not been. We were diverted onto a side railway spur for a brief delay.

As the train slowed to a stop, suddenly I caught an unexpected glimpse of buildings outside. Buildings in the middle of nowhere? I could see a barbed wire fence. Behind the fence sat a few tattered-looking grey barracks. At length I noticed people walking on the colorless, frozen earth behind the wire. As we rolled to a halt, we drew abreast of the nearest group of them.

I had trouble understanding what I was seeing.

Pale grey and white skeletons, walking around. Their thin, thin bodies, their drab, cold eyes sent a shiver through me that chilled me to the soul. They each wore a yellow armband with a black six-pointed star on it. Jews.

My mind leaped and lunged about madly. Whispered rumors came rustling back through my ears. So this was one of the camps! The camps some said didn't exist, the camps others told unbearable stories about. They were real, these camps. They were rumors no longer. They existed. I heard whispers around me, but not one person in that train car could speak aloud.

Though it seemed an eternity, we were not halted there long. The train was soon rolling across normal scenery again. My mind would not leave that sudden encounter with absolute horror so quickly, though. I heard my mother's voice from the year before, asking me about the rumors. "Do we really do such things?" And I had assured her it couldn't be true, that it was all enemy propaganda.

But it was true. I had evidence now. The war had a terrible, secret rottenness at its heart. Or rather, I had fresh evidence to add to the horror I felt on my first arrival in Warsaw, nearly three years before. My eyes opened wider on something I desperately wanted not to see. The faces behind that wire filled my waking imagination and my dreams all the way back through Germany. They have never left me. I can see them today. I still do not know what to do, beyond turning away in horror. It is too awful a sight to bear.

Later that day a team of army officers passed through the train with an unusual order. "All nurses must get off at the next station," they said, as they passed by. "You are needed in the field hospitals."

Erika and I looked at each other, stunned. I was a nurse. Erika was not. We had only a moment to say our goodbyes. Then I climbed down from the train and looked at her through one of the windows. I don't remember whether we waved to each other. And as abruptly as that, we nurses all found ourselves a short time later sitting in the back of a roaring, jolting truck, being carried off away from the rail line to a totally new and unexpected destination.

We ended up in Breslau, then a city in Germany. Today it is called Wroclaw, a city in western Poland since the border moved to the west after the war was over. There on the edge of the city we were deposited at a makeshift field hospital.

It didn't look like any hospital I had ever seen. In fact it had been some kind of factory once. The field hospital had been set up inside the gutted walls of the now empty building. Great steel beams

Klara

ran along the sides of the ceiling, tracks for vanished overhead cranes. There were long rows of dirty glass windows up near the roof, many of which had been cracked and broken so cold winter air seeped directly into the makeshift wards. There were no beds. People were laid in rows directly on the cold floors with whatever blankets we could find to put around them.

I spent nearly all my time carrying food to wounded, maimed soldiers. There was no time for more than the most rudimentary medical care, and a shortage of medical supplies anyway. When I wasn't carrying food I was ripping sheets for bandages. I never seemed to stop working. I hardly got any sleep. I spent so much time on my feet that they became painfully swollen. At night I had to sleep without taking off my boots because I knew I never would have been able to get them on again the next morning.

It could have been worse for me, though. I didn't have to dispose of the ones who died. With the level of care we were able to give, there were plenty who did die. This awful death rate, coupled with the flood of new arrivals pouring in all the time, dictated that some of the soldiers had to simply shovel the corpses out into the icy cold. There the bodies froze solid and so did not begin to foul the air. It was a hideous place. I really have no idea how long I was "imprisoned" in that field hospital. Time was a wandering refugee in those days along with the rest of us. It may have been days, or it may even have been a week or two before I finally was ordered onto a Red Cross train because of my own deteriorating condition, and swept back further into Germany.

This time we got as far as Berlin before I have any clear recollection of my disjointed flight. But Berlin was being bombed all the time now, so we had to get off the train there. In fact we had to get out of the train station itself. We ran out into the broad avenue outside, the great facade of the bahnhof towering above us, its famous row of round windows now already shattered by the concussion of bombs. The street overflowed with people. The wail of air raid sirens filled the air. We ran down into a bomb shelter near the station, a crowd of strangers in ones and twos, as the first bombs began to explode in the distance. The sound came echoing over the roofs of the buildings outside.

The trouble with these bomb shelters was that whenever the sirens began to howl, there always seemed to be more people nearby than the shelter could hold. When it was full the doors were simply closed on the rest.

Just after the door was closed, in the crowded, electric bulb yellow air of the shelter, a woman began to cry. Before anyone knew what was happening she was screaming uncontrollably. I could barely see her, away off on the far side of the shelter. She was so overcome with some private horror and anguish that her screaming was impossible to understand at first. But someone finally made out some words in her screams. The story quickly ran through the underground room.

She had run down into the shelter when she heard the sirens, her precious little baby wrapped up tight in a blanket in her arms. It wasn't until the doors were closed and the bombs were already crashing and exploding in the streets over our heads that she discovered to her horror she had only the blanket in her arms. The baby had slipped out somewhere along the way. That was when she began screaming her despair. She ran wildly, helplessly, from one person to the next shrieking about her baby. Several people tried to talk to her and then to hold her, to restrain her, but she was wild and frenzied with grief, terribly strong in her panic.

Finally some men, unable to restrain her, began to hit her to stop her screaming. They couldn't stand it any longer, so they just hit her until she stopped and lay sobbing on the floor. After that no one could speak to anyone else. No one could even look anyone else in the eye. All were overcome with their own private guilt and horror at what had happened. While the bombs continued, the crowded little room below ground was perfectly still except for the sobs of the grieving mother.

When the raid was over I climbed slowly back up into the cold night air. I walked back to the train station alone, full of sorrow for the woman and the baby. Full of sorrow, too, for the hearts of those men who had battered her into silence. I waited alone for my train. I can't remember the rest of the trip at all, which means it must have been blessedly quiet. The things I seem to remember from those awful days are horrible, tragic memories. I could have done without them all.

Chapter Eight
ASHES ACROSS THE SKY

It must have been early in 1945. I arrived on a morning train. Somebody woke me, and I was surprised to find I was in Melsungen. Only a handful of us got off. People's cold-weather clothing reflected how badly the war was going, bright colors faded, coat edges frayed. Faces had the same dull color as the clothing. I walked up the side of the hill through wisps of snow swirling in the wind. I had to stand on the front steps and shiver in the chill winter air. No one was home.

The forced labor camp still sprawled along the far side of the street, buildings shut against the cold. No way to tell if anybody was in them, except for thin blue curls of smoke coming from little metal chimneys. I waited like that, watching the camp buildings, until at last Mama came trudging up the hill. She had been down to the center of town to pick up her rations.

We went inside and talked most of the afternoon over cups of strong, hot wheat coffee. Hilda was still gone, living and working at an orphanage which seemed to grow after every air raid. But later in the evening, my youngest sister Aline came home from her job in a bank in Melsungen. She had finished her year of national service on a farm, and then been assigned to work in the bank.

"But now we can worry about the rest of them together!" she said, when she discovered me sitting with Mama in the kitchen.

I had to report that I was home again, in case they should want to give me a new assignment. To be found at home without reporting would be desertion, even though the Luftwaffe had first deserted me in Bielany. Deserters were shot on the spot, no questions asked. That was a drastic solution, but effective and easy to enforce. No bother with court martials or other legal processes.

So I walked down to the town hall one morning, accompanying Aline on her walk to work. I gave my name and showed my military passport. I walked around a bit, but there was nothing to buy in any stores and I had no money anyway, so I soon went back home.

Then one night I had a dream, a very peculiar, overpowering dream. It was so realistic I wasn't sure when I first woke up that it had been a dream.

I see a building, tall, made of grey stone, set back from the street. Its façade is mostly screened from sight by a tall iron fence with shiny black bars. A big iron gate, part of the fence, swings inward so I may pass through.

I walk through a dark hallway. It must be inside the building. I come through the open doorway at the end of the dark hall, into a long bare room.

It looks like a barracks. There are windows in long side walls at regular intervals, and three more windows across the far end of the room. White, colorless light pours in through the windows, but the room does not feel warm at all.

Then I see the room is not empty. Two rows of coffins are placed along either wall, where bunks would stand in a normal barracks. Along the center aisle formed by these rows of coffins, on the end of each of them a girl is sitting. As I come in they all turn and smile at me.

I walk part way into the room and look about uncertainly. No one says anything. Finally I blurt out, "Why are you all sitting here on these coffins!?"

"Because they are our coffins," a girl says suddenly, cheerfully, behind my back. I jump at the sound of her voice, and turn around as she explains, "You see, we're all going to die." Another macabre smile. "And then they'll put us in these coffins--"

And I woke up. For a minute I didn't realize the roomful of coffins was gone. When I got my bearings enough to realize it had been a dream, I lay still in the darkness for a moment. I listened to myself breathing, felt my heart pounding in my chest. The comforting weight of my feather quilt pressed down on me. I could smell its reassuring combination of dusty, stale scents.

When my pulse finally stopped racing, I slowly sat up in bed. I wiggled my feet into my house slippers and padded carefully down the darkened stairs to my mother.

She was sound asleep. When I pulled gently at her covers, she stirred and made a sleepy noise. After a moment she opened her eyes and squinted up at me. I sat down on the bed and told her all about the dream. The part about the coffins startled her; suddenly she was fully awake. After I finished there was a moment of silence.

Klara

Mama and I took dreams very seriously; I remember some nights in Ukraine, when my Omi still lived with us. In our farmhouse there were two large bedrooms at our extreme "German" end of the building, and a door into each from the main room with its great hearth. Mama and Papa slept in one room. Omi (my father's mother) slept in the other with all of us children. This arrangement met with our hearty approval because Omi told us stories from her past life at bedtime.

My grandmother had been the local midwife, among her many talents. When a baby was due, a nervous male relative would come bursting in upon us. We jumped into whatever wagon or buggy or cart had been commandeered for the emergency, raced out to the road, swerved into its rutted course, and went rattling and bouncing down the track as fast as the driver dared to go.

Omi jumped out and disappeared at our destination. We played with any available children. Barring some problem, soon afterwards we gathered to look at the new arrival. It always looked very small and red and upset. We tried in vain to picture this small red creature as one of us.

Due to her reputation, Omi was once called to the bedside of a neighbor who was slowly dying. Omi said he was literally "rotting away" in his bed. There was nothing Omi could do to save him or prolong his life. She concentrated on making his last days and hours pleasant ones, as free from suffering as possible. Gratefully he promised she would be well-rewarded after he was gone, though Omi protested no payment was needed. At last, comforted by her help in his final moments, the man died.

His widow thanked her sincerely for her help, but made no sign of the promised reward.

A night or two later, Omi said, she was asleep in her bed when this man who had died appeared. He was standing beside her bed, reaching out as if to touch her. He couldn't seem to reach her. His expression was terribly sad.

"Omi! Weren't you frightened!?" we chorused, chills running up our spines in the darkness of the bedroom.

"Oh, no," she replied, "he was only trying to say thank you. It was the only way he had." We all shivered with delight.

This happened a second night, then a third. She decided to go and have a talk with the man's widow. Before she could even begin, the widow poured out her own tale. It seemed her dead husband had also been appearing to her every night. He would stand at the foot of her bed and simply stare at her with an expression of severest reproach, as if he were angry with her.

Omi told of her own visitations, and of the dead man's promise.

"That must be it!" the widow seized upon the story. "How selfish of me! Of course you shall have a reward." She sent one of her sons to fetch some vegetables and a bundle of cloth she had been saving to make into a shirt for the dead man. They discussed the unusual ordeal for a time and then my Omi returned home. The visits stopped. The man was never heard from again. Growing up with such lessons taught me to take dreams seriously.

The morning after my dream about coffins brought a sunny new day much like any other, though. Before long, the dream faded from my thoughts as the affairs of our real lives continued.

By that spring of 1945 the town had become a positively eerie place. At night, of course, you would never have guessed there was even a town there. The blackout was enforced with a completeness only Germans, now driven by fear in the bargain, could have managed. Still, bombs sometimes fell to their targets.

One morning Mama and I had gone down into town on an errand. We were walking home again when suddenly the unmistakable drone of heavy airplanes came to our ears. Almost before we recognized the sound, it grew much louder and two huge, dark green American bombers roared over our heads, appearing as if by magic over the crest of the hill. They were flying lower than usual. I could see clearly the white stars painted on them.

We stood rooted in the middle of the street, staring in astonishment at this apparition in the sky. Before we could even move, the gigantic metal beasts swept over the town and roared away across the sky toward the west, on their way home.

Simultaneously the air was filled with a chorus of whistling as a handful of extra bombs, left over from some larger raid, hurtled toward us. One struck the river and exploded with a crash, sending a geyser of water spouting up into the morning air. Another plunged through the roof of a house on the far side of the river and then did nothing. It was a "dud" and never did explode. A third landed in the road behind us, several hundred meters back into town. The blast shattered windows all around and blew a gaping crater in the cobblestones of the street.

They missed the bridge, the train station, and the railroad line. No one was injured. It was over almost before we could comprehend what was going on. That was the extent of air raids on our little town during the war.

Aline, Maria, Otto, Klara, Hilda, all home on leave, 1945

By early 1945, a person walking about the town met with very few other people on a typical morning. One of the few "men" left in town was Reiner, a young boy of ten or twelve. Reiner wore a baggy army uniform even though he wasn't really in the army. He had shocking red hair but was no relation to the Grauers. His hair was almost as red as the rattling fenders on his old bicycle. He was an official messenger for military orders. We often saw him pedaling here and there with messages for people. The sight of him was enough to freeze most people in their tracks. He was the one who came to the door with the notices that husbands, brothers, sons had been killed. No one welcomed his visits.

Eventually, as it was bound to do, the machinery of the dying Luftwaffe ground to life briefly and produced new orders for me. The representative of the Third Reich arrived at our house and rang the bell on his bicycle. At first I felt the paralyzing chill of fear that he brought me news of death. Would it be Genya? Otto? Papa? All of them had disappeared from the earth as far as we knew. But it was from the Luftwaffe, addressed to me. So I knew it wasn't that.

"For me this time, Reiner?" I asked, taking the papers.

"Yes maam," he answered, dismounting and stepping in through the gate. "They came in this morning from Kassel."

Mama watched from the doorway as I opened the orders.

"This says Bischofswerda," I replied.

"Where is that?" she wondered. "I never heard of it."

"It says I must transfer in Dresden, so it's east again."

Mother sighed. "Oh, God," she said quietly. She shook her head. I could almost see the lines of care growing deeper on her face, resigned and sad.

The orders didn't really say what I was supposed to do when I got there, but by this point in the war I was pretty certain it was another field hospital. There were never enough people to care for the mushrooming armies of wounded, maimed, dying men flowing back from the fronts.

That evening as I packed my small bag we didn't say very much. It was one of the quietest evenings I ever spent. I laid out my nurse's uniform, ready to put on in the morning. We all went to bed.

The next day Mama and I walked to the train station. Not a word was said. My heart was heavy because of the way Mama looked. Soon I found myself clattering eastward across the bleak landscape. The end of winter in a nation nearing the end of a war paints fields and hills and forests in unparalleled dreariness. The ground lay dark and barren, cold against pale grey skies. The train rolled across this exhausted countryside all day, while mostly unseen above masses of clouds, the sun wheeled overhead.

Klara

Eventually, after more rocking and swaying through the darkness, we pulled into the central station in Dresden. I must have fallen asleep for a little while. I don't remember seeing Dresden at all on the way in. By the time I stepped down onto the long concrete runway between the tracks, it was the middle of the night.

The sight that met my eyes in that dark terminal was like a blow in the face. Everywhere I looked, people crowded into every square meter and yet it was eerily quiet. The only sound was that of children crying to their mothers that they were hungry. People sat huddled together in little groups with their bags and bundles. Some just wandered up and down, hoping to get on a train.

I didn't have to wonder where this crush of humanity was going. I knew. Further west into Germany, further from the Russians, who by this time were pushing across the Polish border and into the Reich itself. Not even Dresden, which had once seemed so far back into Germany as to be quite outside the war entirely, was safe any longer.

Over the preceding years of war Dresden had become a sort of haven. There were no military bases, no munitions factories, no substantial military targets at all in the city. Even the antiaircraft guns around Dresden all had been moved away to protect real targets elsewhere in Germany. And ever since the eastern front had begun to crumble, the city had been gradually filling up with refugees looking for safety.

Now that the city was filled to bursting, it no longer seemed safe. These desperate crowds wanted to continue further to the west. In the faces of most I saw a blankness, a numbing fear, a loss of all hope.

There were some soldiers in the crowd, too. It isn't strictly correct to say that Dresden was no military target at all. It was a rail center second only in importance to Berlin itself in the eastern fringe of Germany. So many refugees were stranded, packed into the station and the rest of the city like sardines, because nearly every train passing in and out was a troop train moving the armies in an attempt to hold back the Russian onslaught. The men in uniform also wore a slightly panicked expression. They each wanted to get wherever they were supposed to be before one of the special squads checked their orders and executed them as deserters. It was ludicrous to treat everyone out of place as a deserter; nearly everyone seemed caught in the wrong place most of the time. But the squads were about, enforcing their grim rules.

Suddenly a man stepped in front of me. I recognized him as a young friend of Hans' from Bielany!

"Klara!" he cried. He lifted me in his arms. "What a wonderful surprise! How long will you be in Dresden? Where are you going to be stationed here?"

I explained I was only transferring trains. Looking around the vast interior of the station, I fixed at last on the great schedule board high on the end wall, above all the ticket windows.

Bischofswerda. Bischofswerda. There it was! One of the first stops on the line to Breslau, even further to the east than Dresden, back towards my field hospital in a factory. With my eyes I followed the line on the schedule to the end where the departure times were listed. Only one train left for Breslau all night; it was scheduled for departure shortly after ten thirty. The large clock mounted in the center of the board showed it was already twenty five past ten!

I would have to board at once! I glanced at the board again to catch the track number, then turned to look anxiously down the rows of train tracks to find the right one. Close at hand, people crowded around the Express coach, leaving shortly after my own train, bound west for Augsburg. I wouldn't have to fight any crowds to get on a train heading east.

"Look!" I pointed up at the schedule board. "My train leaves in just a few minutes!"

He took a minute to digest this news.

"Oh, forget about it," he finally advised. "You know, there are quite a few of us from Bielany here in the city. You ought to come and stay with us overnight, at least."

"Well, I don't know. . ."

He could sense I was weakening.

"You can say you were delayed. Everybody is always delayed these days. You can come with me right now over to my barracks. Actually it's a girls' school, but they've closed it and turned it into a barracks for us refugees."

Klara

I was still unconvinced. A funny feeling had begun to build up inside me. I felt I must get on my train.

"No, I'd better not," I decided out loud. "Please tell everyone hello for me, though! Maybe I'll get to see you all again soon."

He was getting a little exasperated with me.

"Oh, wait!" he exclaimed suddenly. "Do you know who's here? Erika is here! She's living with her parents here in Dresden, remember?"

Of course. I had forgotten that Erika was living here now. For an instant, I was completely persuaded to stay.

But only for an instant. Then the feeling inside me burst out like a tidal wave. There was no way to explain that feeling to him then, nor is there any way to explain it now. I had to get on that train!

He had taken my arm. I pulled free.

"I really have to go," I tried to explain. "Please tell Erika I'm sorry I couldn't come and see her. But I just can't help it. I must get on that train." I pointed down the lines just as the shrill whistle of my train blew, twice. I picked up my bag and began running.

"Okay," he called after me, "but you're as crazy as ever, Klara!"

As I hurried toward my runway, a train whistle shrilled again outside in the night where the locomotive was idling. I ran faster. The train wasn't moving yet, but only a trainman was still on the empty runway, about to signal the engine to start. He waved his arm at me.

"Hurry up!" he shouted. He turned and yelled down the track. "There's a nurse coming! Just wait a second!" There was always room for a nurse! Everybody knew the nurse they helped might end up helping them in a field hospital before they knew it.

I ran faster, my bag banging against my leg. The train was jammed with mostly soldiers. I could see them in the aisles inside the coaches as I approached. Some were even standing on the platforms at ends of the cars.

I reached the train at last, all out of breath. Two soldiers reached down. Taking me by both arms, they lifted me up onto the steps of a car near the end of the train. The trainman turned towards the engine and waved.

Even as I set my bag down on the step above me, we began to roll forward slowly. A shudder ran along the train's length. Slowly, jerkily, with many hisses and groans and crashes of iron against iron, it started to move.

I couldn't get any further into the crammed coach, so I stood on the steps. I managed to turn around, exchanging hands on the handrail by my side, and faced back into the terminal. We began to slide away from the sea of people on the station floor. A few lines over, the long row of train cars of the westbound express reached from the edge of the crowd into the darkness ahead of us. People were still crowding into it. As we emerged from under the vaulted station roof into the night we passed its engines. I could hear they were already running.

By fits and starts we slowly gathered speed, clacking and rocking rhythmically to the northeast through the darkened city. I stood looking out at the silent, shadowy shapes of great dark buildings as they slid past us.

At length we began picking up still more speed as the houses became smaller, more scattered. We were reaching the edges of the city and passing out into the night. We had been in motion for less than half an hour, I am sure.

And about then it began.

Sirens began to wail, first one and then others, from a dozen places in the city we were leaving behind.

For a moment the sound carried me back to my father's sleigh, skimming across the fields on a cold Russian winter day, and the howling of the wolves to each other in that white desert landscape. Rolled up in blankets with only our eyes peeking out, we rode across the snow to visit neighbors. Papa had no gun. His only defense against the marauding wolves was a heap of twine balls soaked in kerosene, which he could ignite and throw as blazing meteors into their faces if they came after the sleigh.

"They can't be bombing Dresden," the soldier behind me said incredulously to his fellow. "There's nothing there!"

But they were bombing Dresden.

Not long after the sirens began, great batteries of searchlights began sweeping the cloudy night sky. A futile exercise, for no antiaircraft guns were on hand to shoot at any planes they might catch in their beams.

The marking bombers had already flown through just before eleven, dropping small bombs which sent up brilliant columns of colored smoke and light towering above the darkened city. One of the marker bombs landed in the middle of the football stadium. They were marking the corners of a zone doomed to destruction.

Behind them the real vanguard of bombers came. Wave after wave of them swept across the sky, high up, in and above the great scattered masses of cloud. There was not a single burst of flak to greet their arrival over the target, to disrupt their aim. Dresden was like a practice range. I have never heard such a droning in the skies before or since. The sky seemed to be a solid metal ceiling of airplanes.

Then it rained death and fire down on all the shadowy buildings, and on the families huddled around their baggage in the darkened cavern of the train station, and on the girls' school converted to a refugee barracks. Dresden was being slaughtered.

Our train continued across the open countryside for a few more brief minutes, but then stopped. With all of its train noises stilled, the crashing echoes of exploding bombs drifted clearly across the night to our listening ears.

"Get off the train. Run out into the fields," came the word. "Trains and railroads are targets."

No one needed any further encouragement. Being on the steps already, I was one of the first off. We scrambled through a low ditch beside the tracks and walked quickly across the bare earth of a tilled field. Some distance away, a single line of trees ran parallel to the tracks. We made for it, our shoes crunching through the crust of soil and leaving deep footprints in someone's field. On the far side was a grassy meadow, the tall stems flat and dead against the ground after the winter's passage. But it was firm ground and drier than the field.

I stopped. Looking back toward the train, I could see waves of people picking their way across the fields behind us. I set my bag beside a tree, and then sat down so I could lean back and rest against the trunk.

We were not far at all from the outskirts of the city. Some of the last buildings of Dresden were visible in the distance, even in the darkness. From our seats beneath the row of trees we had a perfect view of Dresden and the night sky above it. For what seemed like ages as we sat in small groups, wave after wave of bombers kept winging across the sky and pouring down their firebombs on the city. The destruction was taking place right before our eyes. No one could talk very much. We were horrified. Almost everyone I could see was a soldier. They were all sitting or lying in complete silence, preoccupied by the unbelievable, unreasonable spectacle.

At first I worried about bombs falling on us there in the field, but as the attack went on it became clear we had gotten beyond the target area. We had escaped. The Augsburg express was the last train to leave Dresden that night. The people I had seen clambering into the coaches were among the only survivors out of the whole great throng I had left behind. The bombardiers lying in the noses of the low-flying marker bombers reported seeing the white cars of the Express pulling out of the station as they flew over. By the time the main fleet of bombers arrived, it too had passed out of the zone marked for destruction, but its margin of survival had been even thinner than our own.

The station itself had been bombed flat. The second wave of bombers destroyed it. Nearly every one of the people I had watched on the crowded platforms had been killed, in the blast of bombs or the collapse of the great curved station ceiling. Some in lower passageways were trapped and drowned in water from shattered mains even as fires began to spread in the main level above them.

After a time the city began to glow. A harsh light rose into the night sky from the fires set by the bombs. A normal city casts a glow in the sky above it but this light was different, fiercer, brighter. The light grew as the fires spread, joined other fires, and captured more and more blocks of buildings.

More clearly than ever, other noises drifted to our ears. The sounds of a great city being killed were terrifying. The droning of the planes, the whistling of falling bombs, and the steady roar of explosions had abated. Only the uncanny glow in the sky and the sounds of sirens and alarms like a terrified, desperate choir singing a long way off remained.

Perhaps an hour later we heard other sirens closer at hand. Firefighting equipment from all the surrounding towns and cities had been mobilized, and went screaming into Dresden from every point of the compass. Another hour or so later, when all the firefighters from miles around had deployed in Dresden to battle the blazes, the bombers returned. Once again the crashing of bombs was heard as they caught the firefighters along with the rest of the city and blasted them into oblivion, too.

By this time nearly all of the sirens and searchlights were dead. Only the noises of the destruction itself reached us. Dresden no longer gave the slightest signs of life as a city. As the fires continued to grow, the light also increased. Eventually it was as bright as broad daylight, except where the trees cast long black shadows away from the city. We were even beginning to feel a warming of the air from the heat of the conflagration. Then the final horror began.

It started as a faint, low noise, nearly unnoticed over the rest of the tumult. But it grew. It was a terrible low howling sound, the sound of an unnatural, hellish wind blowing as if in a storm. No gusts, just a steadily increasing wind.

"It is from the fires," breathed a man beside me softly, speaking to himself. I had heard of such things. I knew vaguely what it meant. Survivors told unbelievable stories about bomb shelters in which the very air had been sucked out to feed the firestorm, suffocating all inside, or about live flame suddenly gushing in through air ducts and incinerating people closest to it. People caught in the streets fell before the fiery blast. The streets themselves melted, so these cinders were stuck fast to the pavement in many places.

I noticed odd bits of leaves blowing along the ground nearby. There was dust in the air, too, more and more as the wind swelled to a real gale. Even the leafless boughs of the winter trees above our heads could be seen swaying before the blast, in the unnatural midnight light cast by the furnace of a city in the near distance.

The wind was getting stronger as the howl of the storm swelled into a terrifying roar. Before we knew it the storm had expanded so the draft being sucked into the inferno that had been Dresden hit us in real earnest. The force of the wind picked up with frightening suddenness.

Then before I knew it, the howling wind was seizing bushels of dirt and sticks and leaves, hurling them through the air at our heads, buffeting us and knocking people over, nearly blowing us along the ground. In the darkness, the air full of flying debris, I could only see ten or twenty meters ahead of me.

I crouched against the ground to get out of the path of flying sticks and pebbles and dirt. Where in the world could I find shelter from this sudden unnatural whirlwind? Somebody near me crawled away into the plowed field on hands and knees. Heading for the train, I thought. Then another started. I found myself scrambling desperately through the soft, crumbly soil, my eyes, my hair, my ears, my nose filling with dust, my whole body battered by the unbelievable fury of the wind.

We were reduced to a field full of frantic, scrambling blind bugs, grasping handfuls of loose soil, bumping into each other blindly, seizing someone's foot or arm accidentally and then letting go again as we pushed our way across to the train. By the time I got there, many people already had taken refuge between the rails, underneath the cars of the train. The wind was a tiny bit less fierce there, and we clutched at each other for dear life, lying as still as we could, a long tangled chain of humanity clinging to survival on the edge of the inferno.

The outskirts of the city by this time were clearly outlined, a small skyline of their dark shapes standing up between us and the yellow orange sea of flames rising from an impossibly large area at the center of the city. I had never imagined a fire could be so massive, so all-encompassing and all-consuming. At frequent intervals flares shot up against that fiery background, as buildings simply exploded into flames. The storm crept further and further outward. The entire center of the city was smothered in its unholy embrace. Only an uneven fringe of outlying areas was to escape total destruction.

Long after the second wave of bombers loosed their reign of high explosives and incendiaries on the roofs below and departed, the holocaust raged on and on. We hardly noticed the arrival of the dawn. The sky itself became lighter on the horizon behind us, away from Dresden, and the shadows cast by the burning city were dissolved.

In the daylight we could see a towering column of grey-black smoke billowing up into the sky above the city. Like the plume from a volcano, the immense cloud of smoke and ash rose vertically to a great height and then was bent off to the southeast by the wind and carried away from the city like a river of death across the skies.

"Ash Wednesday, and no mistake," muttered the man I had been clutching beneath the train through the night. He rolled onto his stomach and regarding me with a complete lack of expression. His real feelings were buried deep inside. Clearly he was a hardened combat veteran. Even such veterans were no match for the slaughter of Dresden, though. With the city still burning fiercely in the background I heard another man next to him talking.

"After this just get me back up to the front," he said. "I'd rather be killed at the front."

Many people were stirring with the coming of the dawn. And then came the daylight bombers. The horrible began to shade into the incomprehensible. What was the point? The firestorm was still burning in a city devoid of military targets except for a few railway lines. By this time the planes were pouring down their loads of death on ashes and corpses, not a living city. The night raids had been terrifying; these daytime raids were obscene. What reasoning could justify such horror? I never understood that as long as I lived in Germany. Today I have heard the story behind it, but it still sounds like a terrible mistake.

In that spring of 1945 the Russians were pounding our armies back kilometer by kilometer, inexorably moving forward at a devastating cost to both sides. On the western front, everyone was catching their breath and recovering from Hitler's last failed gamble. The Battle of the Bulge had raged over Christmas. And a great conference was coming, a meeting for Stalin, Churchill and Roosevelt at Yalta in the Crimean peninsula.

Stalin was always suspicious that the allies would love to watch his communist state and Hitler's nazi state destroy each other. Something had to be done, to prove to Stalin that the western allies were helping to defeat Germany. A massive demonstration of military power on the eve of the conference would help the western bargaining position enormously. If it could be construed as of direct help to the Russians themselves, even better.

The solution was to use allied air superiority to bomb a city into oblivion. Dresden was chosen. The machinery for the attack was all set in motion. Flight plans were drawn, bombs and planes organized, and in early February the final okay went through.

Then the weather interfered. The firebombing was to have come in the last days before the conference. On those crucial days, dense cloud cover made the whole project impossible.

On February 7th the conference began. Stalin blustered and complained. Though the Allies had set in motion a massive ground attack on the western front, there were no results yet. They had no evidence of aid. Stalin won important concessions concerning the postwar settlement of political boundaries and spheres of influence in eastern Europe.

Then, when it was too late to possibly accomplish its only real purpose, the raid on Dresden went ahead anyway. Packed with refugees numbered in hundreds of thousands, a defenseless city was slaughtered for nothing.

At the time, of course, we there on the outskirts of the city knew nothing of such grand designs. Numbed by the awful destruction, we weren't thinking at all. Our minds had stopped. By afternoon we were beginning to remember the more immediate concerns that go with mortal flesh, though. We were getting hungry and thirsty. I don't remember if that was the first day or later. We were there for several days. The passengers from the train eventually fanned out across the surrounding countryside, seeking shelter and water in any houses they could find. Some were deserted, but in some houses and in a little crossroads village or two nearby, local people did let us sleep on floors and gave us water to drink. We knew better than to ask for food. Most of them had none even for themselves. From time to time I made my way back to the train to see if it might leave eventually. Whenever I went there, it seemed there were some other people there. I wonder if some of the passengers even stayed right by the train the whole time.

I looked up over the train, which hid the city itself from view. The gigantic column of smoke still billowing upward, stretching out across the sky. It was as thick and rising as rapidly as ever. The breeze of the firestorm itself was still blowing, though it was no longer a gale out where we were.

Ruins of Dresden after Allied fire-bombing in February 1945

Eventually, though, I got desperately hungry. My head throbbed. My stomach twisted and complained. I was feeling very weak and tired. A few of us decided to go scavenging across the countryside to see if any food could be found. We walked across the fields and meadows for perhaps an hour and eventually came to a little group of empty buildings. It wasn't quite large enough to be called a village. A "crossroads," perhaps. Behind one house, in a patch of sandy garden, we discovered what we had set out to find.

They were only old, rubbery carrots which had lain frozen in the earth all winter, but we dug them out of the soil with our fingers and ate them, pausing only to brush away most of the sand and soil. It wasn't much, but it helped. We set out on the return journey.

I could not say how long I stayed there in the vicinity of that field, watching an immobilized train and the huge column of smoke and ash pouring out of the husk of what had once been a beautiful city. The next thing I can recall with any clarity is the train in motion eastward again. In the late afternoon, as the last fiery rays of the sun began to recreate a memory of the glow of the inferno over the ruins behind us, everybody somehow managed to jam into the coaches and we slowly started forward. Shock, exhaustion, and the enormity of the last few days combined to blanket the cars with a numbed silence as we once more clattered past the field, the tree row where we had camped, this time without stopping. The reality of Dresden was left behind us. Only our memories accompanied us on our homeward journey in that train.

Chapter Nine
STRANGE EVENTS AND LAST DAYS

Bischofswerda was not far at all beyond Dresden. We stopped there well before evening darkness began to fall, the western sky still red behind us. A few people stepped down from the train with me to confront the small station building. Most were refugees from the destroyed city. The soldiers were bound further east.

A lot of people from the little town hurried to meet this unscheduled train when it pulled into town unexpectedly. They believed it had been caught in the attack and destroyed, until we suddenly showed up several days late. For some our arrival wasn't good news. No other train had come through from the west for days, so several local men who were on their way to the front had to climb aboard.

I feared a mob of people might surround me, demanding tales of the destruction wrought on Dresden. I was terrified of having to relive that scene so soon again, describing it in all its grisly detail before the horror of it settled into a memory in my own mind. I put my head down and hurried across the platform, into the small station building. After many days with almost no food, my hunger left me dizzy and exhausted. It was all I could do to move forward, not tripping over anything.

It didn't take many people to occupy that small space. I caught sight of a Luftwaffe officer standing by one of the windows and looking out after the train.

"Hello, sir," I introduced myself to him. "I've just been assigned here. Can you tell me where this address is?"

He glanced at my orders, at the address I showed him.

"I'm sorry," he replied. "I'm not stationed here myself. I was supposed to catch a train into Dresden two days ago. It never came, so here I sit. I'm afraid I'm at more of a loss than you are. At least you're supposed to be here in this town." He gave my papers back. There was a faraway, preoccupied look in his eye.

I walked across to the ticket window, and asked again. The man behind the window gave me an odd look. He pointed out toward the town as he explained how to get to the place where I had been assigned. It was quite close to the station.

I decided to walk over at once. As I approached my destination, though, I began to have an odd feeling. Something about my surroundings seemed strangely familiar, though certainly I never had been in Bischofswerda before. Some kind of memories were stirring. The curious feeling grew stronger and stronger as I neared the end of the street. My new quarters were in quite a large building; perhaps it had been some sort of school before the war.

It wasn't until a soldier swung open the large iron gate for me, though, that I finally made the connection.

It was my bizarre coffin dream come to life!

I stood stock still, a shiver running up my spine, and looked at that gate. It was the same polished black iron. The building was large, made of grey stone, set back from the street just as it should be. The only differences from my dream were the coils of barbed wire strung all along the top of the iron bars of the wall, and the guard. His pea-green uniform marked him as one of the SS.

Reluctantly, I walked through the gate and up the steps, the hairs prickling at the back of my neck.

However the inside was not a long, dark passageway. A simple table, made from rough wood and painted grey, obviously of military origin, sat squarely in the middle of the entrance foyer. Nobody was in place behind it. I stood in front of it anyway for a moment, a dutiful ritual. But when still no one came, I ventured past it and walked carefully toward the back of the house. At the far end of the foyer, curtains drawn, stood a pair of closed French doors. I could hear voices on the other side. After another moment of hesitation I decided to open them and look in.

The dream returned!

The room must have been a greenhouse at one time. The last red rays of sunlight slanted down through many skylights in the ceiling. But now it was a barracks, the same barracks as in my dream. There were the same evenly spaced windows along each wall. Even the rows of young women were there, but instead of coffins they sat on plain army cots. Conversation died away when I entered. Several people turned to look at me standing in the doorway.

I couldn't very well ask them why they weren't sitting on coffins, though that was the first thought that crossed my mind.

"Well, here's another one!" judged a small, redheaded woman standing at the nearest window. "Where in the world shall we put her, now?"

A renewed babble of voices washed across the room, a spirited debate about where I would sleep. I relaxed a bit.

"What do we do besides sleep?" I asked.

"That nobody knows," the redhead declared. "Nobody seems to know we're here."

"Are you a nurse?" I asked her.

"Yes," she replied, moving over and patting the bed. I sat down beside her. "But that's another crazy thing. Two of us are nurses so far, but there's a little of everything here."

She told me of the others. Filing clerks, a cook, several typists, telephone operators. There was no apparent rhyme or reason to it. Some were Luftwaffe, some were Wehrmacht. No one could say why they were here, so close to the front. Orders simply had come through.

"And what about you?" the little redhead inquired curiously. "What were you up to before you got sent here?"

"I was in a radio receiving station in Warsaw," I replied, "but just now I've come from---"

"You mean you came from the Russian front?" cut in another girl from across the room.

"Yes, from Warsaw."

"Well, you're not supposed to be here, then. There was an order yesterday. Anybody who served on the eastern front is not supposed to be here. The others are already gone. They left in a truck for Berlin."

Using a valuable truck to haul a bunch of women back to Berlin struck me as very irregular at that desperate stage of the war. What was going on here, anyway?

"You'd better go and find the Major or someone," said the nurse beside me. "Your being here is some kind of mistake. You'll probably have to leave again. You were all supposed to be gone by this morning."

"Gone where?"

"Home again, I guess. Back wherever you came from."

"I came through Dresden." That startled several of the girls who heard it. "I barely got through. I won't be going back that way!"

"Through Berlin, then."

"In the middle of the night?"

"I guess you'll have to ask the Major."

"Where is this Major? Does he have a name?"

"Probably he does, but we don't know it. The men all just call him 'sir' or 'Herr Major.' You know these SS."

I went in search of the Major, which didn't take long. He was standing over a soldier who was sitting at the grey table in the foyer. He wasn't very tall, only a little taller than me. But he looked extremely fit and healthy, cutting a trim figure in his immaculate uniform. It was the first immaculate uniform I had seen in weeks. In fact, he was a strikingly handsome man. He turned to regard me with his piercing eyes.

"Yes, Fraulein?"

"Herr Major, I just arrived through Dresden." His eyebrows also jumped for an instant at this. "I've been assigned here, but now I've been told I need to leave again, because I served in Warsaw." I showed him my orders and then explained about Bielany.

He read my papers, an annoyed expression coming over his finely chiseled features. Without looking up from the papers, he confirmed the situation.

"As you say, there has been a mistake."

One look at the special seal in the back of my passport was enough for him. He snapped it shut and gave it back to me. "Your orders are cancelled. You may leave at once."

He hustled me straight to the front door, into the evening twilight without the slightest explanation.

"But I don't understand--" I tried to begin, but he cut me off.

"Your orders were all a mistake. Goodbye!" He went back inside and closed the door. As I left the grounds and headed for the train station again, day was ending and darkness was falling. The guard closed the gate behind me with a heavy clang.

Klara

Something about the Major had disturbed me. What was it, exactly? I walked most of the way back to the train station before I could put my finger on it. He had never really looked me in the eye, even when he was talking to me. It was as though he didn't want to see me.

I was hungry and tired, with no place to sleep and no promise of any dinner in sight. They could at least have let me stay for dinner or even for the night! It didn't look like a promising trip home. Thankfully, though, by the time I got back to the train depot the local Red Cross had reacted to the arrival of the train I had ridden on, along with the other people who had come from Dresden. A single small table with some weak soup in a pot had been set up inside the little station building. Although there wasn't much food value at all in that broth, I gratefully drank some.

That was the last I ever saw of Bischofswerda. I'm not even sure how I got home again after that confused evening. I thought back to the peculiar houseful of women many times afterwards, though, trying to puzzle it out. It was not until after the war was over that one day I learned the truth about Bischofswerda. It happened quite by accident.

In 1946, with the war receding into a memory, I took a train bound south along the Rhine. Below us the great river curved slowly along the deep valley on our left. Two men sat directly across from me in the compartment. They looked like any other civilians in this new postwar world, but as their conversation proceeded I couldn't help overhearing that both had been high-ranking officers in the regular army. They were quietly discussing the SS units they had to deal with under Hitler, the private Nazi army.

"None of them would have lasted a week in my command," said one man.

"Oh, I don't know," his companion countered. "They got some pretty good men in the combat units. I mean, they got first pick of everything, after all. Tanks, uniforms, ammunition, and men too. Their biggest problem was they decided they didn't need the rest of the army."

"I wasn't talking about combat units. I meant the scum that ran the security units, and all that. Remember Bischofswerda?"

When he said Bischofswerda, I must have nearly jumped out of my seat. I tried to show no sign of reaction, looking intently out the window at a large coal barge gliding along the river below. I strained to hear the next words.

"I remember it all right," came the response. "That disgusting little weasel pulled a secretary right out of my own headquarters staff, and before I found out about it, it was too late."

"That's the way it always was with him. That charm, the good looks. No one caught onto him until it was too late. Whatever happened to those girls?"

"The Russians got there, and he turned them all over for a government position in the eastern zone. Those poor women! Presents for the Russians. You know, I've heard the ones who lasted long enough ended up all the way back in Siberia."

"No! I didn't know that."

"Just handed them on, from hand to hand like an old book. The guards in the camps kept the survivors for enjoyment, as long as they lasted. One of these women was even returned not long ago! I don't know why, but she came in with all the others they're shipping back to Germany from eastern Europe. They say she looked eighty years old. All washed out. Her eyes always looking down."

I knew the truth at last. I realized why I had been sent to Bischofswerda. The rejection of anyone who had fought against the Russians made sense. Such a combat record would blemish the "goods" being assembled as a bribe for the incoming Russians. Those girls really had been sitting on their coffins, after all. My dream had been a truer picture than the waking scenes of my visit.

"And did he get the job in the eastern zone? Is he there now?"

"I don't know. I hope they shot him. It's what he deserved."

Silently, I added my agreement to this last judgement.

But when I first got home from Bischofswerda, all I knew was that I was out of a job again. I waited, half expecting Reiner to come pedaling up the hill and ring his bell at our gate, but no new orders came. Russian armies poured across the Polish borders everywhere. British and American armies were driving into the country from the west. Germany was shrinking away rapidly with each passing day.

Klara

The Luftwaffe was so shattered that they lost track of me altogether. I never got another written order from the Third Reich. Its last official word to me was the summons to Bischofswerda, a bitter last word.

But I was not destined to sit in Melsungen to the end. It was a season for dreams, seemingly. It was completely dark in my room, so dark that at first I wasn't sure my eyes were open, and blinked them experimentally. What had wakened me? I thought I had heard Mama call me—once, sharply—as she always did in the morning when it was time for breakfast. But why was it so dark?

I got up. Had I only dreamed that she called me? I opened my door and looked down the stairs. The whole house was dark. It was plainly still the middle of the night.

But I could have sworn someone called me. I padded down the stairs, turned the lights on, and went into my mother's room. She was sitting up in her bed, wide awake. Something had awakened her, too.

"What are you doing up, child?" she asked.

I asked her if she had called me. She had not. I told her I had not called her either.

"Something has happened to someone," she decided. The trouble was that it could have been anyone. Otto, Genya, Papa, all were in danger of one sort or another, all absent. We talked a little while and then she sent me back to bed.

A day or two later the telegram came. The very night of our dream, Otto had been racing along a dark highway on his motorcycle with a dispatch. He hit a mine. It exploded and threw him through the air into a ditch. The machine was destroyed. His side was punctured by shrapnel. Two of his fingers were severed when the motorcycle crashed down beside him. A little closer, and he would have been killed instantly.

For five years Otto led a charmed existence. He survived the invasion of Norway. He even survived Stalingrad. But his luck was running out along with all the rest of Germany. After lying dazed by the road all night, he was discovered the next morning by a search party sent out to recover him and his dispatches. They took him to a makeshift hospital in a small town near Leipzig.

"Oh, my," I said, when I read the telegram. Leipzig. Leipzig was bad. The Russians were sure to capture that whole area very soon.

Mother looked at me without a word. Aline put down her towel and left the dishes to join us at the door.

"That would be the end for Otto. They would never take care of him properly," I voiced all our fears. I couldn't bring myself to suggest they would probably just wipe out the whole place full of wounded Germans as too much trouble for an advancing army to deal with. I gave the telegram to my mother, and announced, "I'll go and get him."

"What!?" Aline exclaimed.

I forced myself to act before the idea could be dissected and proved absurd, heading for the stairs to get a blanket from my room. "It isn't far from here. I can be back in a day or two."

Mama didn't say much of anything.

"But you have no orders to go anywhere," Aline called up after me.

"If I don't go, what will happen to him?"

"What makes you think they'll let you take him away?" she retorted. I had to think about that for a minute. I got my blanket and started down the stairs.

"Maybe he could come to the hospital here in Melsungen," I finally suggested. "After all, that's where they would send him anyway, isn't it? I would just be speeding things up if I went to pick him up. I used to ferry wounded men on the trains all the time."

It actually sounded like it might work when I put it like that. Aline insisted she wanted to come along with me. She said I might need her help, and that two would be able to take care of him better and support him if he couldn't walk on his own.

I went down to the hospital in Melsungen where I had worked years earlier. It seemed more like a century had passed since I had walked those halls, but many of the same faces still turned to recognize me. I talked to the head doctor, and he agreed Otto would be transferred home in the normal course of things. He wished me luck and I could see he meant it. Every life he could save helped him get through those awful last days, too.

Klara

Mama began to believe that the wild scheme might work, and she even consented to let Aline come along. We took a train and I was wearing my nurse's uniform, but Aline had to hide in the toilet a couple of times when people came through checking papers.

The Leipzig hospital was in a convent, on a low hill across town from the train station. We got past a guard at the gate, and marched straight into the great building itself.

The confusion and noisy desperation of the trains and stations were things one almost could get used to, but though I had been in these makeshift field hospitals so often, each time the same shock was there again. For Aline it must have been much worse. It was like walking into hell.

Here, too, there weren't enough beds. Soldiers were sitting against the walls or lying on the floors, crowded together everywhere. The human toll of the bloody finale was piling up in countless hospitals on both sides.

We walked up and down what seemed to be endless corridors, asking names, asking if anyone knew Otto. And of course, nobody knew anything about anybody. They had requests of their own, though.

"Please, nurse, have mercy! Kill me!" A man with no legs begged me to kill him.

Others stared into space vacantly, and when I tried to talk to them, many only asked me, "Where are the Russians? Are the Russians coming yet?" In their eyes was only terror.

We walked around a long, long time. We searched the main floor from one end to the other. Then we went downstairs and looked in the hallways and rooms there. We gave up questioning individuals, simply walking about crying out Otto's name.

Then suddenly, just as I called his name again, a man slumped against a wall right in front of me lifted up his face and looked at me with a slow, exhausted kind of amazement.

It was Otto. I was almost stepping on his feet, but until that moment I hadn't recognized him at all. He had his hand wrapped up in his shirt, still trying to comprehend the idea that there were less than five fingers wrapped up there. He only had his rough field jacket over his shoulders. There were a lot of bandages around his left side.

He just lifted up his face, that was all. For a long time he made no other move. Finally he spoke in a quiet voice.

"I can't believe it."

"We've come to take you home."

Otto was in shock. We led him out of the corner where he had been deposited and back up the stairs. Luck was on our side. No aides were around to stop us. We walked straight into the office of the man in charge of the hospital. He turned out to be an army officer.

"Yes, nurse; what is it?" Everyone assumed I was a nurse.

"This is my brother Otto, sir. I'd like to help him get home to the hospital in our town. I've worked with wounded men many times already, and I can be responsible for him. We will cause no problems."

When he saw how it was, the hospital commander gave us an official paper and told us to go quickly. I suppose he recognized that he was giving Otto a better chance by letting him go. He had no shortage of patients remaining. We left the hospital, walking down the hill into town. There was snow on the ground here, but we had the blanket Aline brought all the way from Melsungen, and Otto was almost as warm as if he had had a coat. He was very weak from shock and loss of blood so we couldn't move very fast. At last we reached the train station.

It was locked! Closed for the night, or rather for the afternoon, since the last train had passed but it was not yet quite dark.

"What can we do?" we asked each other. We couldn't sit outside the station all night, so we set off walking beside the rails, heading for the next station a few kilometers down the track. It might be larger and still open, offering us shelter for the night.

About this time I became aware of the thunder. At first I heard or felt just an isolated, low trembling of the air, but soon Otto noticed it too. As we trudged across the open landscape he declared, "That's Russian artillery. The front is moving this way. By tomorrow they could take the hospital and all this area."

Klara

Finally we reached the next station. It was larger, but it was closed too and night had descended on us. It was getting very cold. At a loss for what to do next, we spotted a farmhouse not far from the rail line. It was our last hope. We were all too exhausted to go much further. Together we stumbled across a frozen field in the darkness, dotted with patches of snow and rows of corn stubble. At last, with the cold closing about us, we reached the house.

I pounded on the door.

"Go away!" shouted a man's voice. "We're full."

"We can't!" I shouted back. "My brother is recovering from wounds and the station is locked up! We only want to stay the night!"

The farmer on the other side opened the door.

"You must be Germans," he declared. But he and his family were already very crowded in that little house, and our visit was no great treat for them.

In the end we had no place to sleep. We sat in the stairway leaning against each other, wrapped the blanket around our shoulders, and managed to sleep a little. The next morning Otto was very stiff and sore in his wounds from our awkward sleeping position. Moving around hurt him quite a bit.

The old farmer was up early, however. We discovered he had his horse and wagon ready. They took us along with a group of other people, all fleeing from the advancing Russians. We rattled across the countryside, our numbers growing with several little stops, until the wagon finally arrived at a large train station. This one was open. The booming of Russian artillery in the distance was much louder this morning, a low continuous throbbing noise just over the eastern horizon, very unnerving.

No train ran according to any schedule by that point. Our luck held, though. A long train rolled into the station late in the morning, already pretty full of people. The mob on the platform pressed forward desperately, seeking places. By some miracle Aline and I pushed Otto ahead of us and managed to squeeze into one of the cars. It helped that I was wearing a nurse's uniform.

At least half of the people on the platform didn't make it, and were left rushing about desperately as the train slowly started up again and pulled out of the station. Shouting and crying filled the air all around us. The three of us just held onto each other for dear life, and I said a fervent prayer of thanks that we had made it.

We came back to Melsungen what seemed like months later. Actually it couldn't have been more than a couple of days, I suppose. Otto was placed in the hospital there in town, where he spent the last weeks of the war.

The collapse was just about complete. All that was needed was for someone to come along and knock down the last few cards still standing, and all the elaborate plans of the Third Reich would be gone from the face of the earth, leaving only their nightmare reminders behind.

Klara

Chapter Ten
HOMECOMING

Springtime itself had to struggle against the hollow grayness of that dreadful last year of the war. Food was scarce. We were always hungry, but we were fortunate to have two chickens and a goat. Our diet revolved around their milk and eggs, plus dried beans soaked and cooked as many ways as we could imagine. Sometimes we had a bit of cabbage. Aline would pick green leaves. There was never any meat.

People were absent from homes all over town. They were fighting at the front, or else they were dead, in hospitals, or simply missing, their condition unknown. Our family experienced all of these except death. Perhaps we were luckier than most in that way. Papa was still fighting on the Russian front, and he had never been wounded yet. Otto convalesced in the hospital. Genya remained missing, his whereabouts unknown. None of the women in the family had been hurt at all. Hilda was working away from home in an orphanage, and Aline and I were at home with Mama.

Since I was at home, I could visit Otto every day. I could hardly avoid it, for I had started working at the hospital again. He asked me about our family every day, and one day asked about my husband.

"So when will I get to meet this Russian fellow of yours?" he asked me.

My first wedding anniversary was nearly at hand. Otto still had never met Genya. I still had no word from him myself. When he jumped back into the armored car and roared away across the countryside, he had disappeared from my life.

"He's Latvian, not Russian. I don't know what's happened to him," I answered. "He might be dead. He might be a prisoner. Or he might step down from the next train pulling into Melsungen."

The day finally came at last, as I suppose we all knew it must. The landscape which had survived almost unchanged for all of the war until then, finally felt the burden of armies locked in the final struggle. The war came to Melsungen.

It was Good Friday, early in the afternoon. I went to work as usual but the hospital guards told me the building was closed. They sent me home, so I couldn't even visit Otto. As I was walking back toward the river, several huge grey-tan tanks, mottled with dark camouflage paint and black German crosses, roared past me and clanked across the highway bridge over the Fulda. I followed them across the bridge. They struggled up the wooded hillside and over the crest of the ridge, northeast of town. Several truckloads of infantry troops followed. The soldiers jumped down to the pavement on the east side of the bridge.

They did not have long to work. Only an hour or two after the first German tank rumbled over the cobblestone streets, we heard the strange, muffled report of a tank gun, followed immediately by a crashing explosion far away on the western slopes leading down to the Fulda.

Mama and I hurried upstairs to peep out of the bedroom windows looking down onto the town. Perched on our own hillside, we saw drab green enemy tanks roll out through the clouds of dirt thrown up by the first shot. All the guns on the enemy tanks began to swing toward the source of that shot, like the trunks of a parade of elephants all swinging in unison. They ground to a halt, spaced out along the slope of the hills. A second shot ripped across the valley, this time landing directly on an enemy tank. There was a blinding explosion.

We fled from the window back downstairs as the enemy tanks began to fire back. Shells whistled back and forth over the town all evening as the two sides blazed away at each other. Nobody was firing into or from the town, however. When at length darkness fell, the tank duel died away at last. But we no longer felt the least bit safe in our flimsy little house. One hit from a tank, and it would fly apart in splinters.

"Let's go up to the hospital," I suggested. "Surely nobody will turn that into a battleground." This sounded good to Mama, too. We locked our house and trudged up the hill in the gathering darkness.

The familiar hospital grounds seemed bigger and lonelier in the darkness. We made our way to the front doors. They were closed up and locked tight. I pounded and called but there was no response.

"They won't let us in!"
"Now what shall we do, Klara?"

Klara

I didn't want to walk all the way down the hill again. We decided to go to Marta's house on the hospital grounds and see if they could put us up for the night.

Marta's mother opened the door.

"Klara! Maria! Aline! Come in!" she welcomed us, introducing us to little Bernie, a boy of about two. He was Marta's son. She never had married. The father had been a soldier, but he had disappeared in the cyclone of war.

"We have enough beds," Marta volunteered, as we discussed how to arrange the night. "You and your mother can sleep in here with me, and Bernie will sleep with mamma. How's that, mamma?"

Marta's mother agreed. Everyone was nearly overcome by nervous exhaustion after living through the battle all evening. We tumbled into bed in no time.

My head scarcely touched the pillow, however, before an uncanny feeling of anxiety tingled through my body. I stared at the ceiling nervously. Something felt very wrong. I sat up in bed.

"Klara? Is anything the matter?" asked my mother.

I didn't answer. Instead I got up and stepped across to the window. The darkened silhouette of the hospital stood in dim shadow across the lawn. After a minute I went back and sat on my bed again. The feeling of wrongness, instead of going away, was growing stronger.

"Klara?" asked Marta.

"I don't know," I answered. "I just don't feel right."

"You're upset about the tanks shooting over the town," she speculated.

"No, I don't know," I said slowly. "I wish we had gotten into the hospital."

Her forehead wrinkled. She sniffed.

"No, no offense to your house, Marta! I just think we should have gone over there."

"Are you crazy?" she countered. "People have been pouring in there all evening! It's already so packed, people are sleeping in hallways. Here you've got beds and you can get a good night's sleep. And we'll probably need that in the next few days!"

I was silent again for a few minutes.

Then I remembered the steam tunnels. Under the hospital grounds, a maze of tunnels ran from the steam plant to the main building and other structures. One of them ended in the Kiels' basement. Marta had showed me years before. We had peered together into the gloomy concrete passageway as she explained the network of tunnels to me. On the other end of this tunnel, a door led into the hospital basement. I had even seen that other door, set in the wall of a basement hallway over there.

Suddenly my mind was made up. "Mama, I want to go over to the hospital anyway."

Marta sighed in her bed. More foolishness.

"But how, my child?" questioned Mama. "The doors were locked."

"We can go through the tunnel in the basement."

Marta sat bolt upright in bed.

"You are crazy, Klara! Wandering in the steam tunnels in the middle of the night! Why can't you just go to sleep?"

But my mind was made up. Mama didn't argue. I often wondered why she put up no resistance to this harebrained idea of mine. Perhaps she felt uneasy, too. I never asked her about it. She and Aline got dressed again, and finally Marta led us quietly out into the living room and down the narrow stairs into the cellar, where the wooden door of the tunnel broke the smooth surface of the wall.

"Okay, Klara. There you are. I guess I'll see you over there tomorrow." She opened the door for us and handed us their flashlight. We each brought a blanket. We expected to sleep on the floor.

"But you're as crazy as ever!" she called softly after us. The sound of her voice went echoing ahead into the darkness, mingling in my imagination with the echoes of another voice calling the same words after me in Dresden. Marta went back upstairs into the house.

Mama, Aline, and I made our way cautiously through the low tunnel. A few minutes later we found ourselves standing in the basement level inside the hospital.

Klara

Marta had not exaggerated. People were everywhere, along the walls in the hallway, and everywhere else. We walked around for several minutes, looking for a place large enough for the three of us to lie down. It seemed half the town thought of the hospital before we had. We kept walking, each clutching our blankets, until at last we discovered a large empty shower room. The floor was hard and smooth, cold tile, but we were ready to drop. We lay down close beside each other, wrapped our blankets around us, and whispered our goodnights.

I lay awake for some time on the cold hardness of the tile, and was feeling more foolish about giving up the comfortable bed with each passing minute.

All at once the building shook. The halls echoed from a loud explosion, close by. For a moment afterward, complete and utter silence reigned throughout the hospital. Not the slightest sound was heard.

Then gradually, when no further blasts followed the first, some talking began again. No one could sleep after that. People were walking around nervously. Indistinct shadows glided past in the dark. I heard somebody talking about a stray shell. It had landed right on the hospital grounds, apparently.

"Was anyone hurt?" someone asked.

"I haven't heard," the voice replied. "They've gone out to check around."

Wide awake, I decided to go for a walk. Near darkness filled the hall. Forms of people curled up on the floor made for slow, careful going. The light improved as I made my way up the wide stairs to the main level. A light glimmered bravely in the main entrance lobby above. I got to the top of the stairs just in time to see the front doors open at the far side of the wide, empty space of floor. Several people lifted a stretcher in through the door and paused while one foot pushed back, pushing the door shut behind them.

I trembled with sudden foreboding. They struggled closer with their burden. One woman held a covered lantern. Its narrow beam speared down to shine brightly on the stretcher. A deathly pale face. Blond hair, bits of grass and mud in the tangles. Horror prickled at my own scalp. I swallowed hard against a sudden lump in my throat.

The face was barely familiar, but I knew it. The limp form on the stretcher was little Bernie!

"Oh no!" I cried. "Who else was hurt?"

A man, a patient in the hospital to judge from his clothing, looked up at me.

"There's no one else left," he said quietly. "The shell came down through the roof of the house. Landed in somebody's bed, from the look of it. The whole house was blown apart. We couldn't even find any other bodies. Somebody spotted something on the lawn as we were coming back in. It might be a part of someone."

I could not speak. The man dropped his eyes again. I dropped my gaze to the floor as well, as the stretcher bearers headed up the staircase to the second floor with poor little Bernie. I just stood alone in the darkness, rooted to that spot for a while.

At last, I managed to cross to the door and pulled it open just enough to slip out. The darkness had grown deeper, but outlines of the hospital buildings still stood out against the sky, amid the trees. As I feared, one outline was gone. Marta was gone. Blown to pieces. I had talked to her less than an hour before.

First Erika perished in the conflagration of Dresden, almost unnoticed in the midst of that massive, brutal horror. That had been Ash Wednesday, the beginning of Lent.

Now on Good Friday, as Lent drew to a close, Marta also perished. This time from a single, senseless, unintentional stray shell. Why the unholy symmetry of these tragedies, spanning such a holy season?

At last the tears came. I sank down on the cold, wet grass, not wiping them away as their salty trails coursed down my cheeks. Why? Why? I tried to pray for an answer to this awful riddle.

It took a long time for this bitter moment to run its course. Finally I struggled to my feet again, though, and retraced my steps to the basement. Mama had fallen asleep, exhausted. I sat down beside her quietly so as not to awaken her, and sat thinking. Perhaps I dozed off. I can't really remember.

Early the next morning, however, everyone was up, roaming restlessly around the hospital. With the first light the fighting recommenced. Now the crackle of small arms fire drifted up the hill from the town below. A battle for the town and its bridges grew louder as morning advanced. Afraid of more "stray" shells, all the people drew together into the hospital basement. It felt very crowded and oppressive.

I told Mama the story of the tragedy of the previous night. She sat in silence for a moment. I sat down beside her and took both her hands in mine.

"You really have an angel watching over you, Klara," she said at last. "You saved our live again. You should thank the Lord!" She squeezed my hands fervently.

We sat together quietly most of the morning. Voices stayed low and quiet in the hospital basement. As noontime drew near, though, many people began showing signs of hunger and restlessness.

I left Mama and walked upstairs to the kitchen. It hadn't changed much at all. I stood in practically the same spot where, in happier times, one day I contemplated a note in my apron pocket.

This time the kitchen was crowded with people trying to be useful. The hospital staff was trying to get rid of them so they could make a midday meal. I recognized many of them, especially the Sisters. Sister Konstanza was there. She spied me in the crowd.

"Come in, Klara! I'll put you to work!" she called, over the heads of people between us. As I squirmed through the throng, I could see as I got closer that her hair was grayer, her face more lined and tired. Her eyes had lost a bit of the sparkle I remembered. But she circled me with one arm and squeezed me to her, glad to see me. I hugged her, too.

Doctor Thompson walked into the kitchen. When I first came walking up the hill years before, he already worked there. He didn't know me, but just seeing him reassured me somehow. Just now he looked thoughtful, preoccupied. A couple of us glanced at him questioningly.

"Oh, it's nothing," he said, in answer to our glances. "I was just standing outside the front door downstairs. The fighting seems to be dying down. The town is so quiet. I wonder what that means?"

"Could you see anything?"

"Oh, no. Anyway, I think half the town must be up here with us!" A small, wry smile tugged at the corners of his mouth. I was struck by that. It was the first hint of a smile I had seen in a very long time. It relieved a bit of tension for a moment or two. "How can we manage to feed them all?" he asked.

How indeed? We packed an extraordinary number into the dining hall. Patients and staff bustled to and from, setting them steaming bowls of soup. But Sister Konstanza returned from a tour of the building and declared, "We've hardly made a dent! The hallways downstairs seem as full as ever. Everyone is staying in the basement." She peered into the dining area, then went inside to admonish people to eat up and make room for others.

We decided to send a crowd of people to the radio room with their soup, to eat as best they could. They balanced the steaming bowls on knees or chair arms. The throng seemed endless.

"Klara," Sister Konstanza demanded, "you take this kettle of soup down to the basement. We'll never get everybody up here. We'll just have to send soup down to them. I'll get somebody to bring some bowls down after you; when the pot is empty, just come back for more."

I nodded. It was a medium sized metal pot, round with a flat bottom and two large handles near the top on the sides. I lifted it experimentally.

"Can you carry it all that way?" she asked me.

"I think so. It's not too big."

"All right. I'll have the bowls coming right behind you."

I took a deep breath, hoisted the pot off the stove, and made my way out into the hall. Compared to the crush and rush of people in the kitchen, the hall was much quieter. I glanced toward the radio room and saw people inside, but the hall itself was relatively empty.

Fragrant steam from the soup drifted up across my face. Trying not to slosh the heavy vessel, I made my way to the top of the central staircase. There I paused to look down the curve of steps. I started down toward the front doors and the wide entrance lobby. The lobby itself was empty. As I started carefully down the staircase I glimpsed Doctor Thompson again, coming across the great expanse of tile. He must have just come up the staircase from the basement. I was about halfway down the stairs when he reached the bottom step, near the front doors.

Suddenly, with a booming crash, the two thick doors burst open. I couldn't take another step. Doctor Thompson had no time even to look around. Helmeted figures dressed in dirty drab green uniforms and big boots leaped through the doorway. Their bayonetted rifles pointed up, down and to every side. Taut and alert, their eyes swept over the entrance hall. One of them stepped up to Doctor Thompson and tentatively asked him a question in English. The doctor, luckily, was one of the few people in the hospital who could understand. He asked if they were Americans. The soldier nodded. They exchanged a few more words.

The officer signaled with his hand. Americans fanned out through the building like ants. A couple of them came up the stairs straight toward me. I stood petrified. Their boots echoed on the wide marble steps. They stopped a step or two below me and regarded me silently.

These Americans who had burst in through the door, except for the officer who confronted Doctor Thompson, were black men. The two soldiers standing with their rifles a bare meter away were just about the first black people I ever saw. Like all soldiers, their clothes were spattered with mud. They looked tense, tired, very lean and hungry.

After a moment, still without a word, one of the black GIs stepped toward me. Our eye contact never wavered. He reached out, took the steaming pot of soup, silently turned and carried it down the stairs and out the door. Another soldier gave me packages of milk powder, egg powder, and shortening. His companion moved past me up the stairs. Others followed him up.

They searched the hospital from top to bottom. No soldiers. An American conversed again with Doctor Thompson by the front door. Melsungen had been captured. German army units had retreated further east, away from the Fulda River where they had tried to stand and fight briefly. He said we should all go home again to our houses.

This news spread like wildfire through the building. For some reason, though, nobody left. We all sat there like prisoners on top of the hill, crowded into that hospital.

However, at last night began to fall again. The very real and unpleasant prospect of spending another night sleeping on cold, hard hallway floors worked its inevitable magic. People began drifting back down the hill into town in large numbers.

Even though it was getting dark, we noticed one major change as we came down the hill to the street past our house. The Americans had opened up the forced labor camp on the other side of the street, and turned all of the Poles and Ukrainians and other prisoners loose. A big, dark green halftrack bearing a white star on the door sat parked in the exercise yard of the camp, just inside the gate. A few GI's were sitting in it.

The town was full of enemy soldiers and freed prisoners! Nervously, we made straight for our front door, hurried inside, closed the door, and left the door unlocked per our orders.

"Well, the end has come at last," my mother observed. "Now what will become of us?" I couldn't offer much useful reassurance on that score.

We lit a small lamp and looked through the house for food. There was precious little to be found, as we already knew before we began to look. Mama lit the stove and brewed some hot water for grain coffee. There we sat, as the darkness of the night settled all around the house outside. We talked in low voices. I was about to go to bed. We jumped in our chairs at an unexpected knock on the door. On our door!

We looked at each other quickly. Expressions of mixed alarm and blank confusion reflected in each other's eyes.

"I'll go," I said at last. Before I got to the door there was another knock, louder and more insistent.

Slowly, I opened the door and peeped out.

There on our front step stood two large men and a woman. All three came from the forced labor camp across the road. They wore tattered grey clothes and had pale, stern faces. I stared at them dumbly. They contemplated me in return for a moment, and then filed solemnly into the living room where my mother still sat at the table. A burly man, obviously powerful despite his pale features, stepped up to the table. He just stood there looking across it at Mama. Then he reached into the jacket he wore. A weapon!?

When his hand came out again he was holding a very large, brown salami. He dropped it suddenly. It landed on the table with a thud.

Then he turned, still solemn, and walked past me back out the door into the night. The second man repeated this surprising performance, depositing a loaf of bread beside the salami and then making a little bow before he left. Finally the woman stepped to the table and carefully set down four wonderful eggs in a row beside the bread. As she turned to go, a hint of a smile played at the corners of her mouth. No one ever really smiled in that time.

"For Easter," she said in a soft voice, in Russian, to my mother. "And God bless you." Then she too was gone.

Mama and I sat together and looked at the eggs.

"You know they must have stolen them in town somewhere," I observed. Mama nodded. Spoils of war. For Easter.

"Did you know them?" I asked.

"I'm not sure. I may have left them a turnip or a couple of potatoes at the fence. Perhaps this is their way of saying thanks."

The next day was Easter Sunday. We hardboiled the eggs, and ate them with bread and sausage. Two eggs each. It was our Easter feast, and also our way of marking the end of the war. Soldiers and prisoners looted other things, too, not just a few groceries. The American troops prevented really serious violence against us, though. Life in Melsungen amazingly quieted back down at once when the fighting ended. We had to stay in our houses practically all the time. Only soldiers could come and go as they pleased.

The Third Reich flickered and winked out of existence at last. Twelve years, not the thousand Hitler had predicted. Looked at that way it didn't seem like much. On the other hand, those twelve years consumed half of my lifetime to that point. We were a generation who were never young.

The most alarming part of this period came, though, when we learned that Otto was gone from the hospital. Along with all the other soldiers recovering there, he had been loaded on a truck by American soldiers and carted away. Could it be that they were doing just what we had heard in terrible rumors about the Russians? Would he just disappear, never to be seen again?

He was taken to the gigantic internment camp at Remagen, until he could be traced in the captured records and accounted for. Then he was marked off in the Americans' records, released, and came home. He was the first of our missing men to return after the end of the fighting.

Papa's return home finally convinced me it was truly over. He was disarmed and sent home from the front when his unit surrendered. Not long after he returned, he started right back at his job in the parks. Early in the morning he could be heard downstairs while I was still in bed. Dishes rattled as he fixed himself some breakfast, closed the door, and headed for a day pruning shrubbery or planting trees. On such mornings, however brief the moment, sometimes it seemed that the war and all its years of horror and anxiety had vanished without a trace. Such momentary illusions quickly passed, but I welcomed even a hint of remembered peaceful memories.

Schulrabe family in Melsungen –
from left to right: Otto, Klara, Maria, Hilda, Aline, Friedrich

We as a family had managed to survive the war intact! It was not a story many of our neighbors could tell with the same happy ending. Heinz Grauer had been killed fighting in France. I knew firsthand how Marta had been blown up in her bed on Good Friday. And Genya? Where was he?

Every day it preyed on my mind. Was he dead? Had the Russians captured him? There had never been a single word from him, no telegrams, no messenger to tell me he was lost. Nothing! The tension, the worry, was with me night and day.

Papa found refuge in his peaceful outdoor work for the town. He seemed amazed and grateful that he had come home safely from the long years on the Russian front. It took more luck than most men can count on in ten lifetimes, he told me.

Above all, he loved pruning the tall trees which lined the roads leading into town. He would carry his short ladder on one shoulder, walking out of town along the road to work alone in the sunshine. One afternoon, up on his ladder sawing away at a dead limb on a tree, he spied a gaunt, bedraggled stranger ambling down the road on foot. He looked as though he had walked a thousand kilometers. His uniform hung on him in tatters, dirty and threadbare.

"Can you spare a drink of water?" this stranger called to him. Papa waved and nodded, and climbed down from the ladder.

"Ah!" the fellow exclaimed, when he had drunk deep from Papa's water bag. "Say, this is Melsungen up ahead, isn't it?"

"That's right. Are you looking for someone?"

The stranger nodded. He explained that he had been released several days before from the Remagen internment camp. Papa remarked that his son had just come home from the same camp.

This fellow had come looking for his wife.

"What is her name?" my father asked.

The stranger spoke my name.

Papa looked at him for a moment without saying a word. He had never met Genya. Then at last tears welled up in his eyes, those eyes which had seen so much loss, so much suffering. He clasped the young man to his chest.

"You are my son," he said, his voice half choked with tears.

The ladder stayed leaning against the tree. They turned toward the town.

A little later, we saw Papa coming up the street alone. Mama and I were in the front yard. Why was he coming home now? What was wrong?

As he came closer, suddenly for the first time in my life I could see his eyes were puffy from crying. Papa crying! The tears still streamed down his cheeks! Chills shuddered through me. Mama and I froze in horror at the sight of him. What could produce such a sight!?

He came through the gate, too worked up even to say a word. He only looked at us, still crying. His emotion was contagious. Mama, confused and frightened, began to cry too. I also felt the tears welling up in my eyes. There was only one thing that could produce such a reaction now. I didn't need to wait to hear him tell me I was alone again. I stepped toward him, holding out my hands.

"I know what has happened, Papa," I said, as I too began to cry.

"Just come in," he managed to command, through his tears. He led us in the front door. "Sit down," he said. We sat down at the kitchen table, still terribly upset and in shock.

Papa walked across to the door leading to the back bedroom, leading out the back of the house. He opened the bedroom door.

Genya stepped through.

He stood there, looking at me as though he had been in the house for years, as if everything was perfectly ordinary.

"Hello, Klara," he said softly, almost shyly. "I prayed every night that I would see you again, and my wish has come true."

Made in the USA
San Bernardino, CA
09 June 2017